DINOSAURS TO DRONES

Take your advanced students on a simulated dinosaur dig and hone the analytical skills required to think like a paleontologist!

Designed to meet the needs of gifted students in grades 5–6, this award-winning curriculum unit consists of 30 lesson plans structured around an included 26-chapter novel. Based on the author's real-life experiences, your students will join Dorian as he travels from New York City to Montana to participate in a paleontological dig. Employing problem-based learning and Socratic seminars, these engaging lessons give students the space to choose which parts of the lessons they'd like to explore further while encouraging them to investigate change over time, from the age of the dinosaurs to the modern era.

With opportunities for student choice and targeted social-emotional learning discussions embedded throughout, this award-winning unit is a must-have for gifted educators seeking to facilitate active student engagement while integrating an exciting, problem-based learning unit into their curriculum.

Jason S. McIntosh is a Senior Instructional Designer for Goodwill of Central and Northern Arizona. Prior to this, he was a teacher and Gifted Coordinator for 27 years. He has five other STEM-related books designed for gifted or advanced students, all of which have won NAGC's Curriculum of the Year award and have been published by Routledge.

DINOSAURS TO DRONES

Investigating Change and Grit Through Paleontology

Jason S. McIntosh

Designed cover image: Getty Images

First published 2025
by Routledge
605 Third Avenue, New York, NY 10158

and by Routledge
4 Park Square, Milton Park, Abingdon, Oxon, OX14 4RN

Routledge is an imprint of the Taylor & Francis Group, an informa business

© 2025 Jason McIntosh

The right of Jason McIntosh to be identified as author of this work has been asserted in accordance with sections 77 and 78 of the Copyright, Designs and Patents Act 1988.

All rights reserved. The purchase of this copyright material confers the right on the purchasing institution to photocopy or download pages which bear a copyright line at the bottom of the page. No other parts of this book may be reprinted or reproduced or utilised in any form or by any electronic, mechanical, or other means, now known or hereafter invented, including photocopying and recording, or in any information storage or retrieval system, without permission in writing from the publishers.

Trademark notice: Product or corporate names may be trademarks or registered trademarks, and are used only for identification and explanation without intent to infringe.

ISBN: 978-1-032-94537-8 (hbk)
ISBN: 978-1-032-94536-1 (pbk)
ISBN: 978-1-003-57131-5 (ebk)

DOI: 10.4324/9781003571315

Typeset in Chapparal Pro
by Deanta Global Publishing Services, Chennai, India

Access the Support Material: www.routledge.com/9781032945361

Table of Contents

INTRODUCTION 1
STANDARDS AND OBJECTIVES 5

LESSON 1	Conceptualizing Change	11
LESSON 2	Calculating the Consequences	19
LESSON 3	A Trippy Train Trip	27
LESSON 4	Digging into Dorian	33
LESSON 5	The Euphoria of Meeting Victoria	37
LESSON 6	The Impact of Incorrect Inferences	43
LESSON 7	A Cavalcade of Character Sketches	49
LESSON 8	Dino Plinko	55
LESSON 9	Location Matters	63
LESSON 10	Care and Feeding of a Dinosaur	67
LESSON 11	Dreaming Up Drone Duties	71
LESSON 12	From Bone to Stone	77
LESSON 13	Dynamic Deductions	83
LESSON 14	Deciphering a Dinosaur Dilemma	87
LESSON 15	Fighting Fears and Considering Cycles	93
LESSON 16	Reexamining Relationships	97
LESSON 17	Creatures and Careers	101
LESSON 18	Predator Competitors	105
LESSON 19	Hand-Drawing a Hadrosaur	111
LESSON 20	Profile on Prejudice	117
LESSON 21	Designing a Drone	121
LESSON 22	Awesome Idioms	127
LESSON 23	Gyroscopes and Game Plans	133
LESSON 24	Breakerspace Breakdown	137

DINOSAURS TO DRONES

LESSON 25	Searching for Serendipity	143
LESSON 26	Delineating the Denouement	147
LESSON 27	Victoria? Meet Sue!	151
LESSON 28	Half On / Half Off	155
LESSON 29	The Evolution of Dorian	159
LESSON 30	The Grit Games	163
APPENDIX	Dinosaurs, Diggers, and Thieves	167

REFERENCES **263**
MASTER MATERIALS LIST **265**
ABOUT THE AUTHOR **269**

Introduction

Description and Special Features

The *Dinosaurs to Drones* unit was a National Association for Gifted Children curriculum network award winner in 2018 and was designed using the Integrated Curriculum Model (VanTassel-Baska, 2023). The unit is unique in that it also includes a companion novel I wrote called *Dinosaurs, Diggers, and Thieves*, which serves as its backbone. The novel was inspired by a real dinosaur dig I participated in during the summer of 2002 in Malta, Montana. A typical lesson in *Dinosaurs to Drones* is structured in the following way:

- ▶ Review of the previous lesson.
- ▶ Recording major events from the assigned chapter in *Dinosaurs, Diggers, and Thieves* onto a timeline.
- ▶ Whole-group exploration of a concept or topic introduced in the chapter.
- ▶ The provision of two choice activities followed by independent work time.

DOI: 10.4324/9781003571315-1

DINOSAURS TO DRONES

- Students sharing the outcome of their chosen choice activity.
- Assigning the next chapter from *Dinosaurs, Diggers, and Thieves*.

The overall goals of the unit are to help students think like a paleontologist, investigate the physics of drone flight, and explore the connections between change over time and grit. A few of the techniques and strategies practicing paleontologists routinely utilize that were incorporated into the unit include:

- Following the bone trail to locate dinosaur bones.
- Distinguishing between regular rocks and actual fossils.
- Documenting a specimen using a grid.
- Making inferences about fossilized dinosaur bones using the Inverted Pyramid of Inference (Witmer, 1995).
- Reading a cladogram.
- Using vocabulary unique to the field.
- Interpreting dinosaur footprints.
- Etc.

Major concepts regarding the science of drone flight include:

- The history of quadcopters.
- Gyro-stabilization.
- The four forces of flight.
- MEMS (micro-electro mechanical systems).
- Global Positioning System (GPS).
- The future of drone technology.
- Etc.

Special care was taken to provide differentiated options throughout. This included differentiating by content, process, product, interest, and learning preference. In addition, all eight multiple intelligences are addressed. A chart displaying a few examples for each can be found below:

| Visual / Spatial | • Construction of timelines.
• Reading dinosaur cladograms.
• Exploring the geologic time spiral.
• Drawing dinosaur "crime scenes."
• Sketching using a grid. |

Introduction

Bodily / Kinesthetic	• Dino Plinko simulation. • Hands-on experiment with faux fossil. • Building model of a quadcopter. • "Breakerspace Breakdown" activity. • Choice to create a skit.
Logical / Mathematical	• Converting acres to feet. • Investigating the knowledge-doubling curve. • Creating if-then statements. • Using logic puzzles. • Calculating the formula for percent of change.
Interpersonal	• Solving problem-based learning tasks in groups. • Cryptic conversations. • The *Predator Competitor TKO* game. • Discussing real-life scenarios involving prejudice. • *The Grit Games* planning process.
Intrapersonal	• Strategies for making friends. • Dealing with loss. • Six habits of highly organized people. • Dealing with fear.
Naturalist	• Horned toad vs. *Zuul crurivastator*. • Wildlife in Montana. • Apex predators. • Astronomy activities. • Global warming and the dinosaurs.
Musical	• Choice to create a musical. • "Flow" choice activity. • Biography of a musician in the book *She Persisted*. • Choice to create a ballad or poem.
Verbal / Linguistic	• Shared-inquiry discussion. • Thinking-hats discussion. • Foreshadowing. • Antiquities Act discussion. • "Awesome Idioms" activity.

Opportunities for assessment are varied as well. The unit includes a pre-test and post-test to measure growth, daily journal prompts that serve as exit tickets, a wealth of classroom discussions to monitor engagement, and several keystone projects students complete to assess comprehension and encourage creativity.

Before Using the Unit and Novel

Three instructional decisions need to be made before a teacher begins implementing the *Dinosaurs to Drones* unit with students. Please read below for a description of the options available to you and select the most appropriate based on the needs of your students.

How will students read the novel?	The lesson plans were written in a manner that requires students to read a chapter of the novel prior to coming to class each day. The benefit of reading before class is that it provides additional class time for students to complete the learning tasks and process the information together. Options for reading the novel include partner reading, the teacher reading the book out loud to the students, or sustained independent silent reading during class.
In what manner will the students construct their timelines?	Throughout the unit, students will create an ever-expanding timeline outlining the events in the story. The lesson plans require students to work in small groups to review the events from the chapter they read for homework and record major happenings on the group's timeline. The students begin with two sentence strips taped together and add on when needed. Other options for creating or using the timelines include having the students work independently to create their own timelines, using technology to create digital timelines instead of paper versions, or facilitating a discussion by which the class as a whole makes one timeline together.
How will you facilitate the daily choice activities?	This unit includes almost daily choice menus from which all students must choose. The only limitation written into the lesson plans is that at least one person must choose each activity. This is to ensure all content is covered once the share-out process has taken place. Other options include creating your own third option each day, eliminating choice on occasion and having everyone complete the same task, or converting the two "daily" choice options into a larger choice menu that students complete once a week.

Final Remarks

Be prepared to visit the world of dinosaurs with your fifth- and sixth-grade gifted students in more depth than ever before. This is not the dinosaur unit you experienced in second or third grade when you were a child. Not only will you and your students learn to think and act like practicing paleontologists, but you will learn life lessons from the characters in the novel while honing analytical skills to make predictions, inferences, and solid arguments. It is my deepest hope that as a result of this unit, your students' love for science and passion for reading will burn hotter and brighter than ever before. Thank you for welcoming me into your classroom and stay tuned for more exciting curriculum units coming in the future!

Standards and Objectives

Overall Unit Outcomes

The students will be able to:

- Use grit as they acquire the skills of practicing paleontologists.
- Conceptualize the science behind drone flight and anticipate future developments.
- Analyze and evaluate a novel to make predictions and construct persuasive arguments.
- Brainstorm solutions to real-world problems.
- Recognize the impact time has on people, places, and things.
- Acquire strategies for dealing with change in their own lives.
- Create accurate inferences from data and other observations.

NAGC Standards Alignment

(2019 Pre-K–Grade 12 Gifted Education Programming Standards)

- ▶ 1.1. Self-Understanding. Students with gifts and talents recognize their interests, strengths, and needs in cognitive, creative, social, emotional, and psychological areas.
- ▶ 1.2.3. Teachers create a learning environment that promotes high expectations for all children, support for perceived failures, positive feedback, respect for different cultures and values, and addresses stereotypes and biases.
- ▶ 1.5.1. Educators use evidence-based approaches to grouping and instruction that promote cognitive growth and psychosocial and social-emotional skill development for students with gifts and talents.
- ▶ 1.6. Cognitive Growth and Career Development. Students with gifts and talents identify future career goals that match their interests and strengths. Students determine resources needed to meet those goals (e.g., supplemental educational opportunities, mentors, financial support).
- ▶ 2.5.1. Educators provide opportunities for students to set personal goals, keep records, and monitor their own learning progress.
- ▶ 3.1.4. Educators design differentiated curricula that incorporate advanced, conceptually challenging, in-depth, and complex content for students with gifts and talents.
- ▶ 3.1.5. Educators regularly use pre-assessments, formative assessments, and summative assessments to identify students' strengths and needs, develop differentiated content, and adjust instructional plans based on progress monitoring.
- ▶ 3.2.1. As they plan curricula, educators include components that address goal setting, resiliency, self-management, self-advocacy, social awareness, and responsible decision making.
- ▶ 3.3.2. Educators encourage students to connect to others' experiences, examine their own perspectives and biases, and develop a critical consciousness.
- ▶ 3.3.3. Educators use high-quality, appropriately challenging materials that include multiple perspectives.

Standards and Objectives

- 3.4.1. Educators select, adapt, and use a repertoire of instructional strategies to differentiate instruction for students with gifts and talents.
- 3.4.2. Educators provide opportunities for students with gifts and talents to explore, develop, or research in existing domain(s) of talent and/or in new areas of interest.
- 3.4.3. Educators use models of inquiry to engage students in critical thinking, creative thinking, and problem-solving strategies, particularly in their domain(s) of talent, both to reveal and address the needs of students with gifts and talents.
- 4.1.2. Educators provide opportunities for self-exploration, development and pursuit of interests, and development of identities supportive of achievement (e.g., through mentors and role models) and a love of learning.
- 5.1.2. Educators use enrichment options to extend and deepen learning opportunities within and outside of the school setting.

Next Generation Science Standards Alignment

The students will have the opportunity to develop the following scientific and engineering practices listed as important by the Next Generation Science Standards:

- Asking questions (for science) and defining problems (for engineering).
- Developing and using models.
- Using mathematics and computational thinking.
- Constructing explanations and designing solutions.
- Engaging in argument from evidence.
- Obtaining, evaluating, and communicating information.

The students will also work towards meeting the following subject-specific science standards:

- 5-PS2-1. Support an argument that the gravitational force exerted by Earth on objects is directed down.
- 3-5-ETS1-2. Generate and compare multiple possible solutions to a problem based on how well each is likely to meet the criteria and constraints of the problem.

- MS-LS2-2. Construct an explanation that predicts patterns of interactions among organisms across multiple ecosystems.
- MS-LS2-4. Construct an argument supported by empirical evidence that changes to physical or biological components of an ecosystem affect populations.
- MS-LS4-1. Analyze and interpret data for patterns in the fossil record that document the existence, diversity, extinction, and change of life forms throughout the history of life on Earth under the assumption that natural laws operate today as in the past.
- MS-ESS1-1. Develop and use a model of the Earth-sun-moon system to describe the cyclic patterns of lunar phases, eclipses of the sun and moon, and seasons.
- MS-ESS1-4. Construct a scientific explanation based on evidence from rock strata for how the geologic time scale is used to organize Earth's 4.6-billion-year-old history.
- MS-ESS2-2. Construct an explanation based on evidence for how geoscience processes have changed Earth's surface at varying time- and spatial scales.
- MS-ESS3-5. Ask questions to clarify evidence of the factors that have caused the rise in global temperatures over the past century.
- MS-ETS1-2. Evaluate competing design solutions using a systematic process to determine how well they meet the criteria and constraints of the problem.
- MS-LS2-3. Develop a model to describe the cycling of matter and flow of energy among living and nonliving parts of an ecosystem.

Common Core Language Arts Alignment

Conventions of Standard English:

- Demonstrate command of the conventions of standard English grammar and usage when writing and speaking.

Key Ideas and Details:

- Describe how a particular story's or drama's plot unfolds in a series of episodes as well as how the characters respond or change as the plot moves toward a resolution.

Standards and Objectives

Vocabulary Acquisition and Use:

- ▶ Acquire and use accurately grade-appropriate general academic and domain specific words and phrases.
- ▶ Demonstrate understanding of figurative language, word relationships, and nuances in word meanings.

Text Types and Purposes:

- ▶ Write informative/explanatory texts to examine a topic and convey ideas, concepts and information through the selection, organization, and analysis of relevant content.

Research to Build and Present Knowledge:

- ▶ Gather relevant information from multiple print and digital sources, using search terms effectively; assess the credibility and accuracy of each source; and quote or paraphrase the data and conclusions of others while avoiding plagiarism.

Comprehension and Collaboration:

- ▶ Engage effectively in a range of collaborative discussions with diverse partners on grade level topics, texts, and issues, building on others' ideas and expressing their own clearly.

Presentation of Knowledge and Ideas:

- ▶ Present claims and findings, emphasizing salient points in a focused, coherent manner with relevant evidence, sound valid reasoning, and well-chosen details; use appropriate eye contact, adequate volume, and clear pronunciation.

Range of Reading and Level of Text Complexity:

- ▶ Read and comprehend complex literary and informational texts independently and proficiently.

Lesson 1

Conceptualizing Change

Objectives

- The students will complete a pretest.
- The students will generate enduring understandings of the concept of change.

Materials

- Pretest and answer key
- Markers
- Chart paper
- Blank notebook for each student to use as a journal

DINOSAURS TO DRONES

Assessments

- Unit pretest
- Consensus map
- Exit ticket

Procedures

1. Greet the students and introduce the title of the new unit. Ask the students to talk with a partner about what they believe they might learn as a result of this curriculum.

2. Write the words DINOSAUR and DRONE on the board or a piece of chart paper. Challenge the students to find a connection between the two.

3. Explain that many people find this difficult due to the fact they are so different from each other (e.g., one is ancient and one is high tech, one is alive and one is a machine, etc.). Listen to students' ideas and then point out that the two together represent the concept of *change*.

4. Ask students to list any synonyms they know for the word *change* (e.g., evolve, develop, adapt, mutate, etc.).

5. Before moving forward, explain that you would like to know how they personally define the word *change*, as well as what they already know about dinosaurs and drones.

6. Distribute the pretest while making sure students understand that the test is not graded and is meant only as a reflection tool for students and a planning tool for the teacher.

7. When students are finished, collect and score before the next class period.

8. Divide students into groups of four and ask them to work together to duplicate the following consensus map on a large piece of paper (Figure 1.1).

9. Assign each person in the group one of the outside slices and ask them to write their personal definition of change (i.e., the definition for change they wrote on their pretest). There should be no talking or discussion at this point in the process.

Conceptualizing Change

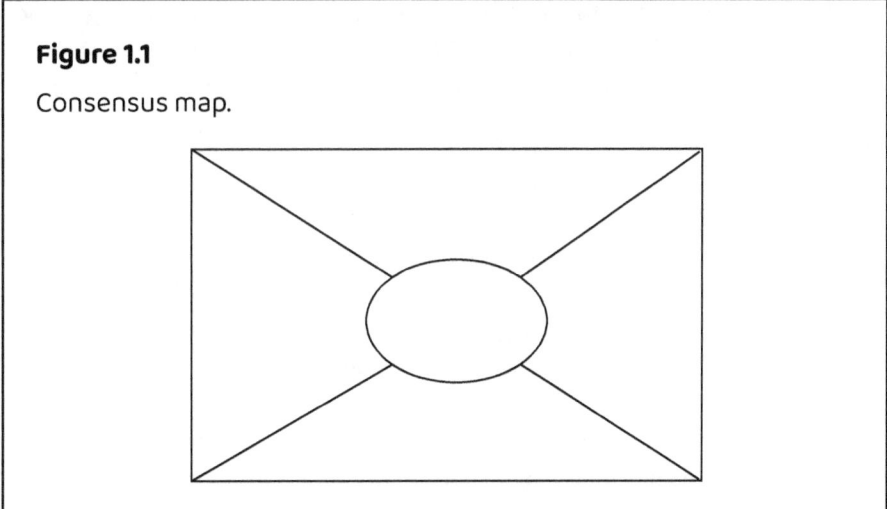

Figure 1.1

Consensus map.

10. Next, set a timer for five minutes and challenge students to (a) share their personal definition with the group, and (b) come to a consensus on a common definition they can all agree on. This should be written in the oval located in the center.

11. Ask each group to share their group definition with the entire class. Work together to create one class definition by combining the individual group definitions.

12. Distribute an empty notebook to each student. Explain that this will be used as their journal throughout the unit. Ask students to open the notebook, place today's date on the top of the first page, and copy the class definition on the first few lines.

13. Provide an opportunity for students to share an example from their own lives of when they experienced great change (e.g., changing schools, moving to a new state, parents divorcing, etc.).

14. Based on these experiences and the new class definition, ask students to list generalizations (also known as *enduring understandings*) they can generate about change. Kick off this conversation by listing the following three examples:

    ▷ Change can happen quickly or slowly.

    ▷ Change can be small or large.

    ▷ Change can be positive or negative.

15. Once again, ask students to record these big ideas in their new journals.

DINOSAURS TO DRONES

16. Preview what is to come by explaining they will be reading a book called *Dinosaurs, Diggers, and Thieves*. The book is about a seventh-grader named Dorian who is undergoing major changes in his life. Read the book description below out loud to the class:

    > Dorian, a young teen from New York City, suddenly finds himself living in the middle of nowhere on a 1,500-acre ranch in Montana. Although nothing like the Big Apple, the small town of Saddle Creek holds more than he bargained for...the fossilized remains of a dinosaur near his new home, a diverse group of quirky neighbors, and a pair of thieves that will stop at nothing to steal the dinosaur at all costs. Join Dorian as he learns the techniques followed by real paleontologists and discovers that you never know what you'll find when you give change a chance!

17. As an exit ticket, ask students to react to the book description using the following prompts:
    a. I think...
    b. I wonder...
    c. That reminds me of...

Name: _____ Date: _____

Pretest

Directions: Answer the questions on this pretest to the best of your ability. This is not for a grade and will only be used to help your teacher better differentiate for you and measure growth.

1. Define the word *change* in your own words below:

2. How do you typically react to change in your own life?

3. Define the word *grit* and provide an example of a time when you personally demonstrated grit.

Definition:	Example:

4. List everything you know about *dinosaurs* and *drones* below. If you need additional space, continue writing on the back.

5. Write the formula for calculating the percent of change in the box below.

LESSON 1

15

Name: _____ Date: _____

6. Label the three main branches of the dinosaur family tree (Figure 1.2).

7. Describe the process of *following the bone trail* in the space below.

8. Label the five parts of the *Pyramid of Inference* (Figure 1.3).

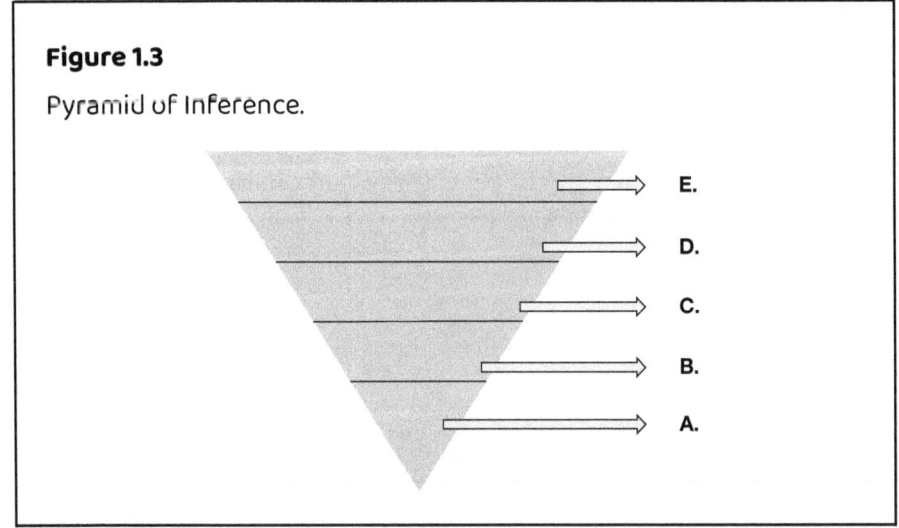

Name: _____ Date: _____

9. List the four forces of flight:
   ▷

   ▷

   ▷

   ▷

10. Describe *gyro stabilization* in the space below.

11. List unanswered questions you have about dinosaurs and drones.

Name: _____ Date: _____

Pretest Key

1. Answers will vary.
2. Answers will vary.
3. Answers will vary, but in general, *grit* is stick-to-itiveness, perseverance, etc.
4. Answers will vary.
5. The formula for calculating the percent of change:

$$\frac{\text{Amount after change}}{\text{Original amount}} \times 100$$

6. Label the three main branches of the dinosaur family tree.
   A. *Sauropods*
   B. *Ornithischians*
   C. *Theropods*

7. Describe the process of *following the bone trail*.

   Walk along the bottom of a hill looking for small pieces of bone. Once a piece is found, stand in the spot facing the hill. Search diagonally up the hill from this spot until the source of the bone fragment is found. Make sure to search diagonally to the right and to the left of the spot where you find the piece.

8. Label the five parts of the *Pyramid of Inference*.
   E. *Community structures*
   D. *Interactions with other species*
   C. *Behavior of dinosaur*
   B. *Function of structure*
   A. *Soft tissue*

9. List the four forces of flight.
   A. *Lift*
   B. *Gravity*
   C. *Thrust*
   D. *Drag*

10. Describe *gyro stabilization*.

    Gyro stabilization is the process of using a gyroscope to keep something from falling over. The spinning of the gyroscope around a vertical axis makes the object resist sideways motion because of inertia.

11. Answers will vary.

Lesson 2

Calculating the Consequences

Objectives

- The students will evaluate a scenario and determine the level of grit it requires.
- The students will research a change event and rate its speed, degree, and quality.

Materials

- *Continuum of Change* Chart graphic organizer
- *Consequence Calculation Investigation* cards
- *Consequence Calculation Investigation* worksheet

DINOSAURS TO DRONES

- *Grit-O-Meter* chart
- *Dinosaurs, Diggers, and Thieves* by Jason McIntosh, Ph.D.

Assessments

- *Consequence Calculation Investigation* worksheet

Procedures

1. Review the class definition of *change* generated previously.
2. Display the enduring understandings of change recorded during the previous lesson. Distribute the *Continuum of Change* chart listed in the materials section to each student. Ask the students to identify how the two correlate.
3. Challenge students to define the words *speed*, *degree*, and *quality* using the pictures found on the chart.
4. If not already included on the list generated during the previous lesson, add that "Change has both intended and unintended consequences."
5. Give the following example:

    Buying a smartphone with a larger screen means you can see the images on the screen more easily, but you might also have to buy jeans with larger pockets in order to carry it.

6. Distribute a copy of the *Consequence Calculation Investigation* worksheet to each student, along with one of the *Consequence Calculation Investigation* cards. Explain that their task is to spend the next 15 minutes (a) researching the change event listed on their card, and (b) answering the questions shown on the *Consequence Calculation Investigation* worksheet.
7. Provide an opportunity for students to share a brief summary of their change event; any unintended consequences; and their ratings for its speed, degree, and quality. Collect this worksheet in order to score or provide feedback at a later date.
8. If not already on the list of enduring understandings, add the idea that "Change often requires grit."

Calculating the Consequences

9. Poll the students to see who knows what *grit* means. Explain that *grit* means *to have courage, perseverance, and determination.*
10. Display the *Grit-O-Meter* chart included in the materials section (Figure 2.1). Ask the students to rate the amount of grit the following change scenarios took to complete:
    a. The United States fighting for independence from Britain
    b. Apple creating the latest version of the iPhone
    c. A baby learning to walk
    d. A school raising money to buy a new classroom pet
    e. Finding a vaccine for COVID-19
11. Ask students to rate the amount of grit it took for the change event they just researched and share this with the class.
12. Remind students that they will be reading *Dinosaurs, Diggers, and Thieves* during this unit. Explain to students that in the novel, the main character Dorian experiences changes in his life that are sudden and transformative, but he also has to solve a mystery that requires high levels of grit.
13. Read chapter one of the novel using one of the methods listed below:
    a. Instruct students to read chapter one independently before the next class period.
    b. Read the chapter out loud to students.
    c. Provide class time for the students to read it with a partner or on their own.

Name: _____ Date: _____

Continuum of Change Chart

SPEED OF CHANGE		DEGREE OF CHANGE		QUALITY OF CHANGE	
	Sudden		Transformative		Delightful
	10		10		10
	9		9		9
	8		8		8
	7		7		7
	6		6		6
	5		5		5
	4		4		4
	3		3		3
	2		2		2
	1		1		1
	Slow		Just a Tweak		Dreadful

Directions: Record the speed, degree, and quality of change for various change events when prompted by your teacher. Refer to the rating scales above to help calibrate your responses. Keep this in a safe place, as you will be using it throughout the unit.

Date	Event	Speed	Degree	Quality

Name: _____   Date: _____

Consequence Calculation Investigation Cards

Consequence Calculation Investigation JACKIE ROBINSON BECOMES A DODGER IN 1947	**Consequence Calculation Investigation** NEW COKE INTRODUCED IN 1985	**Consequence Calculation Investigation** HURRICANE KATRINA HITS LOUISIANA IN 2005
Consequence Calculation Investigation WORLD WIDE WEB INVENTED BY TIM BERNERS-LEE IN 1990	**Consequence Calculation Investigation** YURI GAGARIN ENTERS SPACE IN 1961	**Consequence Calculation Investigation** ZUCKERBERG LAUNCHES FACEBOOK IN 2004
Consequence Calculation Investigation WALL STREET CRASH OF 1929	**Consequence Calculation Investigation** THE MOVIE *JAWS* RELEASED IN THEATERS IN 1975	**Consequence Calculation Investigation** FORD'S MODEL 'T' GOES ON SALE IN 1908
Consequence Calculation Investigation SONY'S WALKMAN GOES ON SALE IN 1979	**Consequence Calculation Investigation** APPLE'S iPOD GOES ON SALE IN 2001	**Consequence Calculation Investigation** PEARL HARBOR ATTACK IN 1941
Consequence Calculation Investigation RAY KROC OPENS THE FIRST MCDONALDS IN 1955	**Consequence Calculation Investigation** SCIENTISTS MAP THE HUMAN GENOME FOR THE FIRST TIME IN 2003	**Consequence Calculation Investigation** BARACK OBAMA ELECTED PRESIDENT IN 2008
Consequence Calculation Investigation	**Consequence Calculation Investigation**	**Consequence Calculation Investigation**

Name: _____ Date: _____

Consequence Calculation Investigation Worksheet

Part I Directions: In the chart below, record how life existed before the change, during the change, and after the change.

Before the change…	During the change…	After the change…

Part II Directions: Think carefully about the change event you researched. Rate the change event according to each scale from 1 to 10.

Rate the **speed** of the change brought on by the event:									
1	2	3	4	5	6	7	8	9	10
Slow									Sudden

Rate the **degree** of change to society brought on by the event									
1	2	3	4	5	6	7	8	9	10
Just a Tweak									Transformative

Rate the **quality** of the change brought on by the event:									
1	2	3	4	5	6	7	8	9	10
Dreadful									Delightful

Name: _____ Date: _____

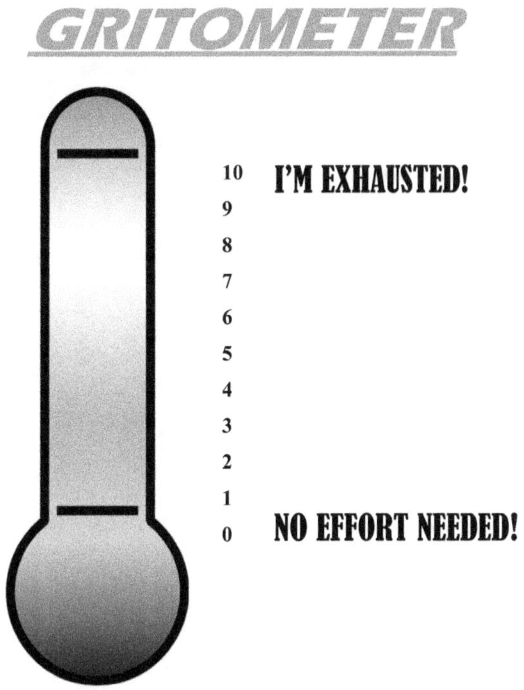

GRITOMETER

10   **I'M EXHAUSTED!**
9
8
7
6
5
4
3
2
1
0   **NO EFFORT NEEDED!**

Figure 2.1 Grit-O-Meter.

Lesson 3

A Trippy Train Trip

Objectives

- The students will rate the degree, quality, and speed of change experienced by the main character of the book.
- The students will calculate mathematical conversions between feet, yards, and acres.

Materials

- Chapter one of the book *Dinosaurs, Diggers, and Thieves*
- *Continuum of Change* chart
- Calculators

- Two or more yard sticks
- Four rulers
- Student journals

Assessments

- *Continuum of Change* chart
- Journal responses

Procedures

1. Welcome students back to class.
2. Explain how the lessons during the rest of the unit will be structured:
    - The students read a chapter from the novel.
    - The class discusses what occurs and then completes an activity together.
    - The students select a choice activity from a menu to complete by themselves.
3. Review the list of enduring understandings and the definition of *grit* discussed during the last class session.
4. Instruct students to find a partner and summarize the major changes Dorian is going through in his life in chapter one (e.g., leaving New York City, moving to a small town in Montana, finding out he has a mysterious great-uncle he didn't know existed, etc.).
5. Ask students to pull out the *Continuum of Change* chart given to them during the previous lesson. Instruct students to record and rate these changes separately in two or three of the empty rows below the chart.
6. Conduct a whip-around using the question below. A whip-around is a sharing strategy in which each student provides their answer to a question one at a time without any breaks or comments between answers:

    If I were Dorian, I would feel...because...

A Trippy Train Trip

7. Remind students that chapter one takes place on an Amtrak train like the one shown below (Figure 3.1). Poll the students to see if anyone has ridden on a passenger train such as this. Ask those who have to talk briefly about the experience.

Figure 3.1

Amtrak train.

8. Tell students that there are over 160,000 miles of train tracks crisscrossing the United States alone. Explain that it all began with the completion of the transcontinental railroad in 1869. Challenge the students to rate the amount of grit this accomplishment must have taken using the *Grit-O-Meter*.

9. Ask the students if anyone has been to Montana before. If so, ask them to share a little about the topography, climate, etc. Display the picture of an actual ranch in Montana shown below (Figure 3.2). Challenge students to find a partner and discuss the three questions below as they examine it closely:
   ▷ What do you notice in the picture?
   ▷ What do you think about when looking at this picture?
   ▷ What questions come to mind when you look at this picture?

Figure 3.2

Ranch in Montana.

10. Show students the second picture of the same ranch (Figure 3.3) and ask that they list anything that surprised them. Is this what they pictured when the word *ranch* was mentioned in chapter one?

Figure 3.3

Ranch in Montana.

A Trippy Train Trip

11. Provide an opportunity for students to share any questions, highlights, or revelations they have about chapter one.
12. Explain to students that they will now be presented with two choice activities. They will have the remainder of the period to explore the one that interests them most. The only rules for choice time are:
    ▷ A minimum of two people in the class *must* choose each task.
    ▷ Students must remain focused and work collaboratively.
    ▷ Students must stay in the struggle and use all of their available resources before asking the teacher for help.

CHOICE A	
Materials:	• Journals • Computer with internet access
Directions:	The fictional town of Saddle Creek in the novel was based on a real town called Malta, Montana. Please go to the Amtrak website (www.amtrak.com/home) and determine the cost and duration of a train trip from New York City to Malta, Montana. Record this information and create a map of your chosen route in your journal.
Assessment:	You must be able to: a. Explain why you planned a pretend trip to Malta and not Saddle Creek b. Share the final cost and duration of your trip c. Display the map you created of your chosen route

*Note: It may be helpful to give your students a quick tutorial on how the Amtrak site works before they begin.

CHOICE B	
Materials:	• Journals • Several yardsticks *and* rulers • Calculator (*at your teacher's discretion*)
Directions:	The ranch Dorian is moving to is 1,500 acres. An *acre* is a term that originated in old English and meant "an open field." It was considered to be roughly the size a farmer could plow in one day. In today's terms, we can visualize the size of an acre by thinking about a football field. A football field is about 1⅓ acres. A typical Walmart is 2 to 2½ acres. Make a prediction as to how many square feet are contained within 1,500 acres and record this in your journal. After your prediction, use the yardsticks and rulers provided to calculate how many square feet are in one square yard. Record this in your journal. Lastly, if there are 4,840 square yards in one acre, how many square feet are in 1,500 acres? Compare this to your prediction. How close were you?
Assessment:	You must be able to: a. Calculate how many square feet are in 1,500 acres b. Explain how you determined your answer

DINOSAURS TO DRONES

13. At the conclusion of the independent work time, ask both groups to share what they discovered. The sharing component is important because it will allow each group to teach the other about what they discovered. Please make sure those who chose activity B know the correct answer is 1,500 × 4,840 × 9 = 65,340,000 ft^2.

14. Preview the chapter by explaining Dorian will arrive in Saddle Creek and meet a new friend. Ask students to complete the following prompt in their journals:

    I think Dorian's parents didn't tell him about his great-uncle because...

15. Read chapter two of the novel to the students, or ask that it be read independently before the next class period.

Lesson 4

Digging into Dorian

Objectives

- The students will participate in a shared-inquiry discussion to debate whether the main character in the story might be gifted.
- The students will assess their own social skills and identify their own strengths, interests, and weaknesses.

Materials

- Chapter two of the book *Dinosaurs, Diggers, and Thieves*
- Sentence strips
- Tape
- Student journals

DINOSAURS TO DRONES

Assessments

- Student-created timelines
- Journal responses

Procedures

1. Review material covered during the previous lesson (e.g., how to convert feet into yards and acres, the terrain of the ranch inherited by Dorian's family, etc.).

2. Divide the students into small groups. Provide each group with four individual sentence strips. Ask them to lay the strips end to end and tape them together to form one long rectangle. Next, ask students to reconstruct the following diagram on their new strip:

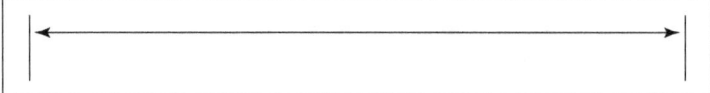

3. Explain to the students that they will be documenting major events from the novel in chronological order using this timeline. The far left represents the beginning of the story. The far right represents the end of the story. Show students several examples of other timelines found online.

4. Set a timer for five minutes and ask students to record major events from chapters one and two on the left-hand side of the timeline. Remind students that there are many more chapters to go and they should therefore leave room. Additional sentence strips can be added at any time if students run out of space.

5. Pull the students back together and ask them to share what they recorded for chapter two (e.g., Dorian arrives in Saddle Creek and meets Tom and Eric, etc.).

6. Work together as a class to list what we know about Dorian's strengths, weaknesses, and interests so far.

7. Conduct a Socratic seminar using the steps below:
    a. Ask each student to write down in their journals the answer to the following question: *"What evidence is there to show that Dorian could be gifted?"*

Digging into Dorian

    b. Arrange students in a circle and explain the process:
- This is fundamentally a debate without one right answer.
- Students will take turns sharing their answers to the question in no particular order.
- The teacher will facilitate the discussion but not offer his or her thoughts and opinions.
- At any time, anyone in the circle can ask for evidence from the text to back up an opinion they have doubts about.

    c. Share the rules for the discussion listed below:
- Be respectful towards each other.
- Disagree with ideas and not people.
- Allow everyone a chance to speak.

    d. Begin the discussion. Remember, the teacher should only ask questions.

    e. After the discussion has gone 10 to 15 minutes, stop the students and ask them to go back to their original answer. Do they still believe what they initially wrote down or did someone change their perspective?

8. Provide an opportunity for students to share any additional questions, highlights, or revelations they have about chapter two.

9. Explain to students that it is now choice time. Remind them of the rules introduced during the last class period:

    a. A minimum of two people in the class *must* choose each task.

    b. Students must remain focused and work collaboratively.

    c. Students must stay in the struggle and use all of their available resources before asking the teacher for help.

CHOICE A	
Materials:	• An interest inventory or multiple-intelligence survey • Journals
Directions:	Earlier in today's lesson, you generated a list of Dorian's strengths, weaknesses, and interests. Complete the interest inventory or multiple intelligence survey your teacher will give you now. Record your own strengths, weaknesses, and interests in your journal based on these results.
Assessment:	You must be able to share a personal strength, interest, and challenge.

*Note: Various inventories and surveys are available online for free.

CHOICE B	
Materials:	• Sentence strips • Tape
Directions:	Create a timeline of major events in your own life. Ideas you might include are instances when: (a) you moved, (b) a new baby brother or sister was born, (c) you won a competition or achieved a goal, (d) you broke a bone, (e) you took a memorable vacation, etc.
Assessment:	You must be able to share three of the events you included on your personal timeline and why they were important to you.

10. After 15 or more minutes, debrief the results of the choice activities by asking students to share.

11. Instruct students to complete the following journal prompt:

    Which domains might you be gifted in (e.g., verbal, quantitative, nonverbal, music or art, leadership, etc.)? How do you think being gifted in these areas has impacted your life?

12. Read chapter three of the novel to students, or ask that it be read independently before the next class period.

Lesson 5

The Euphoria of Meeting Victoria

Objectives

- The students will read a cladogram to determine which branch of the dinosaur family tree a hadrosaur belongs to.
- The students will analyze a historical document and apply it to a current situation.

Materials

- Chapter three of the book *Dinosaurs, Diggers, and Thieves*
- Student timelines
- *Paleontology Lexicon Log* handout

DINOSAURS TO DRONES

- Small wooden dinosaur skeleton model with the pieces scrambled
- Highlighter
- Copies of the Antiquities Act of 1906 for each student
- *Continuum of Change* Chart
- Student journals

Assessments

- Timelines
- Journal responses

Procedures

1. Review big ideas from the previous lesson (e.g., Dorian's strengths, weaknesses, and challenges, major events from chapter two, etc.).
2. Ask students to work with their groups to add important events from chapter three of the novel to their timelines.
3. Provide an opportunity for students to share.
4. Remind students that Dorian was curious about what Tom did for a living in chapters one and two. Now, it has been revealed that he digs up dinosaur bones. Ask students to name this type of scientist (i.e., paleontologist).
5. Explain that the word *paleontology* comes from Greek and Latin. It translates to "the study of what is ancient." Poll the students to see if anyone knows why scientists regularly use Greek and Latin root words. Make sure students understand that Greek and Latin used to be common languages and became the language of science in part due to the work of Carl Linnaeus. Furthermore, Latin is a dead language, which means it is stable and does not change.
6. Give students several minutes to research Linnaeus and the two-part naming system he created called *binomial nomenclature*, which is used to classify all living things.
7. Pull students back together and ask if anyone recalls what type of dinosaur Tom and Eric discovered (i.e., a hadrosaur or duck-billed dinosaur). Display a picture of a hadrosaur and ask students what they notice about it.

8. Explain that dinosaurs have family trees just like humans. Paleontologists call these family trees *cladograms*. Pass out the *Paleontology Lexicon Log* and ask students to define this word in row one.

9. Draw the diagram shown in Figure 5.1 on the board and ask students to recreate it in their journals:

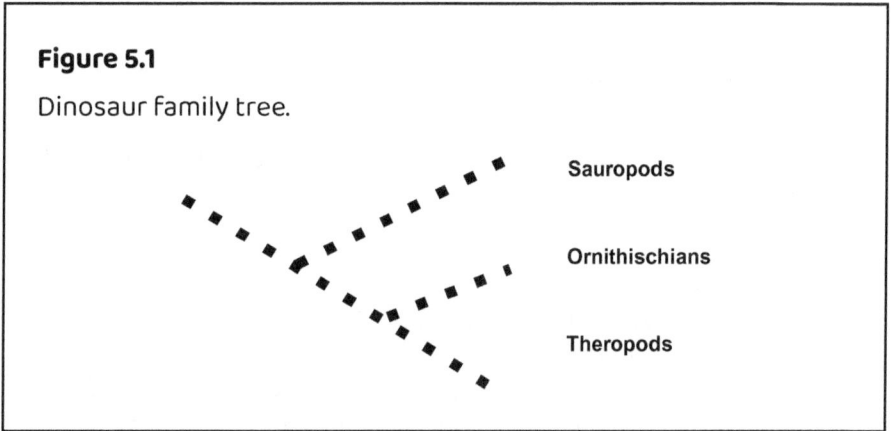

Figure 5.1

Dinosaur family tree.

10. Ask students to define the three Greek words above on their *Paleontology Lexicon Log* as well:
    ▷ *Sauropodomorpha* = lizard-footed forms
    ▷ *Ornithischia* = bird-hipped
    ▷ *Theropoda* = beast of prey or beast foot

11. Challenge the students to predict what the differences are between the three branches of the dinosaur family tree based on the meaning of these words. In general, *sauropods* walk on four legs, have long necks, and eat plants; *ornithischians* have beak-like mouths, eat plants, and walk on either four legs or two; and *theropods* have sharp teeth, hollow bones, sharp claws, walk on two feet, and eat meat. Explain to students that they will learn more about the three groups later in the unit.

12. Next, ask the students to guess which branch of the dinosaur family tree a hadrosaur came from after examining the picture displayed during step seven once more (i.e., ornithischia).

DINOSAURS TO DRONES

13. Explain that cladograms are not based on DNA but are constructed by analyzing the body structure of different dinosaurs. This means they are subject to change. For example, a major revision to the dinosaur cladogram was proposed as early as March 2017. The article "Dinosaur Family Tree Poised for Colossal Shake-up" by Sid Perkins appeared in *Nature* magazine on that date. The article can be found at the following link:

    http://www.nature.com/news/dinosaur-family-tree-poised-for-colossal-shake-up-1.21681

14. Ask students to go back to their *Continuum of Change* chart and log the possible shake-up in the dinosaur family tree.

15. Provide 20 minutes for the students to engage in the choice activities described below:

CHOICE A	
Materials:	• Small wooden dinosaur skeleton model puzzle • Journals
Directions:	Can we know for sure what hadrosaurs truly looked like? Write what you think in your journal. We do know that the dinosaur Tom found was *articulated*. Define this word and record it in your *Paleontology Lexicon Log*. Use the dinosaur model your teacher will give you to demonstrate the differences between articulated and unarticulated dinosaurs. Check with the teacher to see if you were correct.
Assessment:	You must be able to: a. Share your answer to the question posed b. Demonstrate the difference between articulated and unarticulated dinosaurs

CHOICE B	
Materials:	• Copy of the Antiquities Act of 1906 • Journals
Directions:	Tom used to work for the Museum of the Rockies. Go to their website and explore the type of work they do: https://museumoftherockies.org. We know that Tom and the town cannot dig on federal land without permission. Read through the copy of the Antiquities Act of 1906 that your teacher will give you. Write down in your journals anything that pertains to Tom's situation.
Assessment:	You must be able to: a. Describe the type of paleontological work conducted by the Museum of the Rockies b. Share how the Antiquities Act of 1906 applies to Tom

16. Pull students back together and ask each student to share what they learned from the activity they chose.

17. Ask students to complete the following journal prompt:

    What would you do if you were Bill, Susan, and Dorian? Would you let Tom and Eric continue to dig on your property? Why or why not?

18. Read chapter four of the novel to students, or ask them to read it independently before the next class period.

Name: _____ Date: _____

Paleontology Lexicon Log

TERM	DEFINITION

Lesson 6

The Impact of Incorrect Inferences

Objectives

- The students will understand how paleontologists use inferences to draw conclusions about extinct dinosaurs and then make inferences themselves.
- The students will research geologic time and the history of life.

Materials

- Chapter four of the book *Dinosaurs, Diggers, and Thieves*
- Timelines
- Student journals

DINOSAURS TO DRONES

Assessments

- Journal responses
- Timelines

Procedures

1. Review material covered during the previous lesson (e.g., branches of the dinosaur cladogram, important components of the Antiquities Act of 1906, etc.).
2. Ask students to work with their groups to add major events from chapter four of the novel to their timelines.
3. Provide an opportunity for students to share.
4. Pose the following discussion question to the class: "If dinosaurs lived millions of years ago, how do we know so much about them? What evidence do we have that they existed?" (e.g., "We have found fossilized bones, footprints, droppings, eggs," etc.).
5. Explain that because dinosaurs were around before recorded history, we have to use clues to infer what life was like when they were around. Review the definition of the word *inference* with students before proceeding (i.e., "a conclusion reached on the basis of evidence and reasoning").
6. Display the diagram in Figure 6.1 and ask students to reproduce it in their journals.

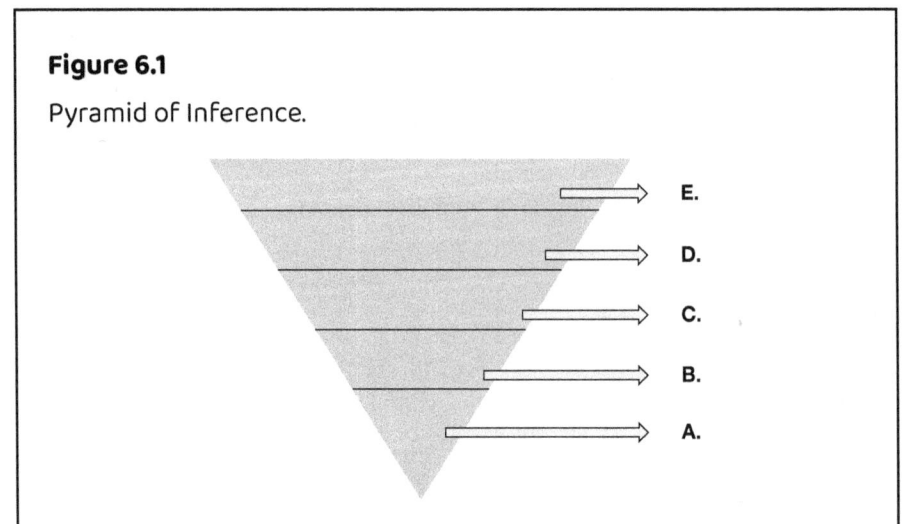

Figure 6.1

Pyramid of Inference.

The Impact of Incorrect Inferences

7. Label the diagram "The Pyramid of Inference" (Witmer, 1995).
8. Ask the students to imagine that the tip of the pyramid rests on the visible, concrete evidence that we have to show dinosaurs existed (e.g., bones, footprints, eggs, etc.).

    The bones we find are pretty easy to interpret and take few inferences to understand.

9. Instruct the students to label section A on the right side of the pyramid as *Soft tissue*. Ask the students what they think soft tissues are (e.g., cartilage, skin, muscle, tendons, etc.). Explain that very few soft tissues of dinosaurs remain. Because of this, scientists have to make educated guesses about what these looked like and how they layered over the bone. These educated guesses are inferences that we may find out are wrong one day.
10. Instruct students to label section B on the pyramid as *Function of structures*. Ask the students what they think this might mean. Explain that because we cannot observe a dinosaur walking or moving, we have to infer what each body part was used for and how it functioned.
11. Instruct students to imagine that our educated guesses about the soft tissue were wrong. How would this impact our inferences about the function of these structures? Quite obviously, they would be wrong as well.
12. Ask students to label section C on the pyramid as *Behavior of dinosaurs*. Explain that paleontologists make inferences about how dinosaurs behaved from the inferences they made about their structures and soft tissues. Once again, ask how accurate these conclusions would be if the inferences made at levels A or B were incorrect. The first mistake is compounded because future inferences are based on erroneous information.
13. Repeat the process by labeling D as *Interactions with other species* and E as *Community structures*. D refers to how dinosaurs of different species interacted with each other. E refers to family structures between dinosaurs of the same species (e.g., courting rituals, who cared for the young, etc.).
14. Pause and take questions while also clarifying any misconceptions.
15. Provide time for students to share any other questions, revelations, etc., regarding chapter four of the novel.

DINOSAURS TO DRONES

16. Provide 20 minutes for students to work on the following choice activities:

CHOICE A	
Materials:	- Geologic time spiral, or other graphic outlining geologic time - Journals
Directions:	Locate the geologic time spiral or other graphic outlining geologic time. One sample resource is the link below: https://commons.wikimedia.org/wiki/File%3AGeological_time_spiral.png. Discuss with a partner what you notice about the spiral (e.g., periods are combined to form eras, organisms become more complex over time). Remembering that the concept for this unit is change, how does this graph represent change in a meaningful way? Record your observations in your journal.
Assessment:	You must be able to: a. Share two original observations about the time spiral b. Describe how the time spiral represents change in a meaningful way

CHOICE B	
Materials:	- Books about dinosaurs - *Paleontology Lexicon Log* - Journals
Directions:	Philip called his ranch Cretaceous Ranch. Dorian did not know what it meant and decided to research it later. You will now do the same. Research the answers to the following questions and record your answers in your journal: a. What does *Cretaceous* mean? b. What is *geologic time*? c. What are the three *periods* of time in which dinosaurs lived?
Assessment:	You must be able to: a. Share your answers to the questions asked b. Help anyone who did not choose this activity record the definition of *Cretaceous* in their *Paleontology Lexicon Log*

17. Give each group time to share what they discovered. The answers to the questions posed in choice B are as follows:

   a. *Cretaceous* literally means "chalk." The Cretaceous period is considered to be 145–166 million years ago. Many types of dinosaurs and the first flowering plants flourished during this time. It ended with a mass extinction (*DK Knowledge Encyclopedia: Dinosaurs*, 2014).

The Impact of Incorrect Inferences

    b. *Geologic time* is the history of life recorded by fossils in rocks and divided into periods (*DK Knowledge Encyclopedia: Dinosaurs*, 2014).

    c. Dinosaurs lived during the Triassic, Jurassic, and Cretaceous periods.

18. Ask students to complete the following journal prompt:

    In the last lesson, I asked you to predict what Dorian and his family would decide about allowing Tom and Eric to carry on with their work. Were you correct? List the inferences you made in order to come to this conclusion.

19. Read chapter five of the novel to students, or ask that it be read independently before the next class period.

Lesson 7

A Cavalcade of Character Sketches

Objectives

- The students will distinguish between fact and opinion to draw their own conclusions and make predictions.
- The students will generate a list of tools paleontologists use and explore one in depth.

Materials

- Chapter five of the book *Dinosaurs, Diggers, and Thieves*
- *A Cavalcade of Character Sketches* handout

DINOSAURS TO DRONES

- Timelines
- *Paleontology Lexicon Log*
- Student journals

Assessments

- Journal entries
- Timelines
- Character sketch handout

Procedures

1. Review material covered during the previous lesson (e.g., the Pyramid of Inference, the definition of *Cretaceous*, the geologic time spiral, etc.).
2. Ask students to work with their groups to add major events from chapter five of the novel to their timelines.
3. Provide an opportunity for students to share.
4. Distribute a copy of the *Cavalcade of Character Sketches* handout to each student. While doing this, ask if anyone knows what *cavalcade* means. Define the term as "a series or procession." Next, explain that a character sketch is a short piece of writing that describes a person's behaviors and personality traits.
5. Remind students that we were introduced to six new characters in chapter five. Ask students to complete a character sketch of each one using the handout by:
   a. Rereading the descriptions provided by Eric and classifying each piece of information as fact or opinion.
   b. Making inferences based on these facts and opinions.
6. Once students have finished, discuss their predictions together as a class.

A Cavalcade of Character Sketches

7. Provide 20 minutes for students to work on the following choice activities:

CHOICE A	
Materials:	• *Paleontology Lexicon Log* • Computer • Journals

Directions:	In your journal, create a list of tools and supplies you believe paleontologists need on a dig site. One tool you might not have heard of is called a *Brunton*. Conduct a search online to learn what it does and fill in the blanks below:
	
	    A Brunton is different from a traditional compass because it measures _____ and _____.
	
	Record this definition on your *Paleontology Lexicon Log* and then answer the second question below in your journal:
	
	    Why do you think it is important to measure the position of a fossil before moving it?

Assessment:	You must be able to:
	  a. Share several of the tools on your list
	  b. Help anyone who did not choose this activity record the definition of Brunton on their *Paleontology Lexicon Log*
	  c. Explain why paleontologists record the original position of a fossil before removing it

CHOICE B	
Materials:	• Computers • Journals
Directions:	Scientists follow a specific process called the scientific method. List the steps of the scientific method in your journal. Cryptozoologists are quite different from traditional scientists. Research what a cryptozoologist is and list three things they might study. Create a Venn diagram or double bubble map in your journal comparing a traditional scientist with a cryptozoologist.

Assessment:	You must be able to:
	  a. List the steps in the scientific method
	  b. Discuss the diagram you created comparing a scientist and a cryptozoologist

DINOSAURS TO DRONES

8. Give students time to share what they discovered. The answers to the questions posed in choice A are as follows:

    a. The words that fill in the blanks are *strike* and *dip*.

    b. The reason it is important to document the exact orientation and location of a fossil before moving it is this may provide valuable clues that may be lost.

9. Ask students to complete the following journal prompt:

    If I were a cryptozoologist, I would want to become an expert in _____ because _____

10. Read chapter six of the novel to students, or ask that it be read independently before the next class period.

TEACHER NOTE:

There are many opportunities to develop creativity when exploring cryptozoology. Consider offering the following enrichment opportunities to students to complete in their free time:

▶ Students randomly select three animals and then combine them to form a new cryptid. Next, they write a story or poem about how it was discovered.

▶ Students choose a famous cryptid and design a zoo exhibit that the creature could live in.

▶ Students read a legend or myth about a cryptid and adapt it into a screenplay or musical.

Name: _____ Date: _____

A Cavalcade of Character Sketches

Directions: Think about the descriptions of each character provided in chapter five. Categorize this information as fact or opinion and then make three inferences by answering the questions that follow.

Character #1
<u>Jose</u>

Fact _____ Opinion

My Inferences

a. Importance of this character:
   (1 = not important to 5 = important)
       1   2   3   4   5

b. Accuracy of Eric's opinions:
   (1 = not accurate to 5 = very accurate)
       1   2   3   4   5

c. My opinion of this character is:

Character #2
<u>Sylvia</u>

Fact _____ Opinion

My Inferences

a. Importance of this character:
   (1 = not important to 5 = important)
       1   2   3   4   5

b. Accuracy of Eric's opinions:
   (1 = not accurate to 5 = very accurate)
       1   2   3   4   5

c. My opinion of this character is:

Character #3
<u>Alexander</u>

Fact _____ Opinion

My Inferences

a. Importance of this character:
   (1 = not important to 5 = important)
       1   2   3   4   5

b. Accuracy of Eric's opinions:
   (1 = not accurate to 5 = very accurate)
       1   2   3   4   5

c. My opinion of this character is:

Name: _____ Date: _____

LESSON 7

Character #4 Cassandra	Character #5 Mr. Connor	Character #6 Zade
Fact ──────── Opinion	Fact ──────── Opinion	Fact ──────── Opinion
My Inferences	***My Inferences***	***My Inferences***
a. Importance of this character: (1 = not important to 5 = important) 1 2 3 4 5	a. Importance of this character: (1 = not important to 5 = important) 1 2 3 4 5	a. Importance of this character: (1 = not important to 5 = important) 1 2 3 4 5
b. Accuracy of Eric's opinions: (1 = not accurate to 5 = very accurate) 1 2 3 4 5	b. Accuracy of Eric's opinions: (1 = not accurate to 5 = very accurate) 1 2 3 4 5	b. Accuracy of Eric's opinions: (1 = not accurate to 5 = very accurate) 1 2 3 4 5
c. My opinion of this character is:	c. My opinion of this character is:	c. My opinion of this character is:

Lesson 8

Dino Plinko

Objectives

▶ The students will begin a problem-based learning scenario designed to help them learn how practicing paleontologists follow the bone trail.

Materials

▶ Chapter six of the book *Dinosaurs, Diggers, and Thieves*
▶ Dino Plinko game (Follow the DIY instructions link provided ahead of time)
▶ Two pieces of Elmer's foam board

- Scissors or knife
- Glue
- Toothpicks
- Bottle lid or poker chip
- *Need-to-Know Board* handout
- *Welcome Packet* handout
- Timelines
- Student journals

Assessments

- Journals
- Timelines
- *Need-to-Know Boards*

Procedures

1. Review major content introduced during the previous lesson (e.g., what a character sketch is, the purpose of a Brunton, how a scientist is different from a cryptozoologist, etc.).
2. Ask students to work with their groups to add major events from chapter six of the novel to their timelines.
3. Provide an opportunity for students to share.
4. Explain to students that the choice activities section of the lesson will be suspended for the next few days. Instead, the class will engage in a problem-based learning task in small groups.
5. Begin by asking the students to summarize with a partner and then in their journals what it means to *follow the bone trail*.
6. Check for understanding by asking a few volunteers to share what they wrote. Correct answers should include the following:
   a. Walk along the sides, near the bottom of a coulee.
   b. Look for bits of fossils that have tumbled down the hillside.
   c. If one is found, trace it up the side of the hill until you find the source.

7. Pose the following question for students to answer as a class: Why would there be small pieces of fossils at the bottom of the coulees anyway? (Answer: Erosion uncovers fossils buried in the Earth and gravity pulls the pieces down the hill.)

8. Poll the students to determine who has ever seen the game show *The Price is Right*. If they have seen it, ask how many know of the game called Plinko, which is periodically featured on the show. (Note: Clips of people playing Plinko can be found online.)

9. Use Plinko as an analogy for how bone fragments make their way down a hill. Construct a classroom-scale Plinko game using Elmer's foam board, glue, and toothpicks ahead of time. See the example in Figure 8.1. Instructions can be found online in various places, one of which is: www.happinessishomemade.net/diy-backyard-plinko-party-game/.

Figure 8.1

Plinko game.

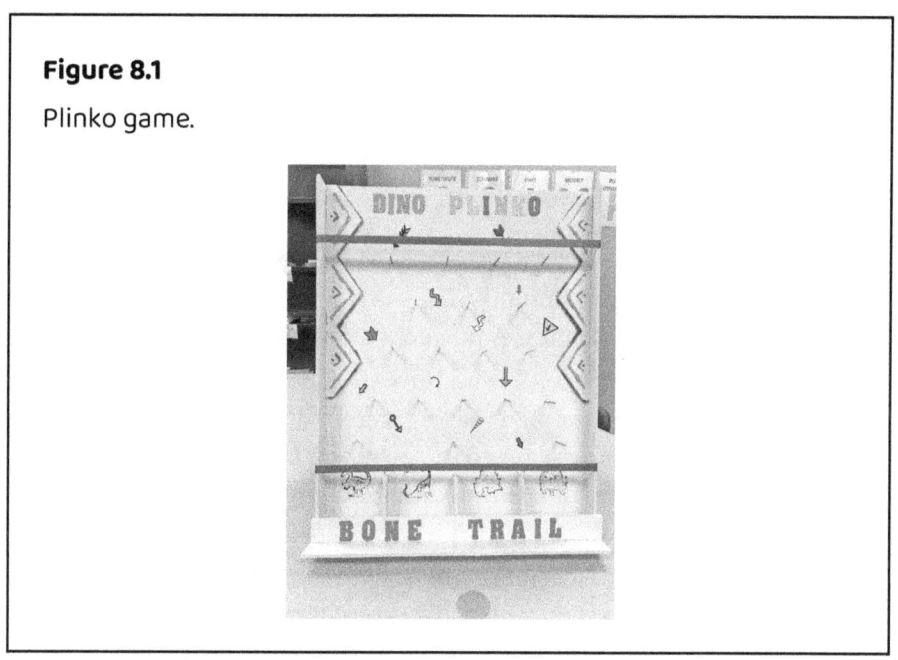

10. Instead of point values at the bottom of the board, place pictures of various dinosaurs. Make sure to include only one theropod (e.g., Tyrannosaurus, raptor, etc.).

11. Place the chip (e.g., a bottle lid, poker chip, etc.) at the top of the board and let the students watch the chip fall to the bottom. Explain that gravity pulls it downward, and it collides with toothpicks on the way down. Students should notice that it falls in a slightly different way each time (Figure 8.2).

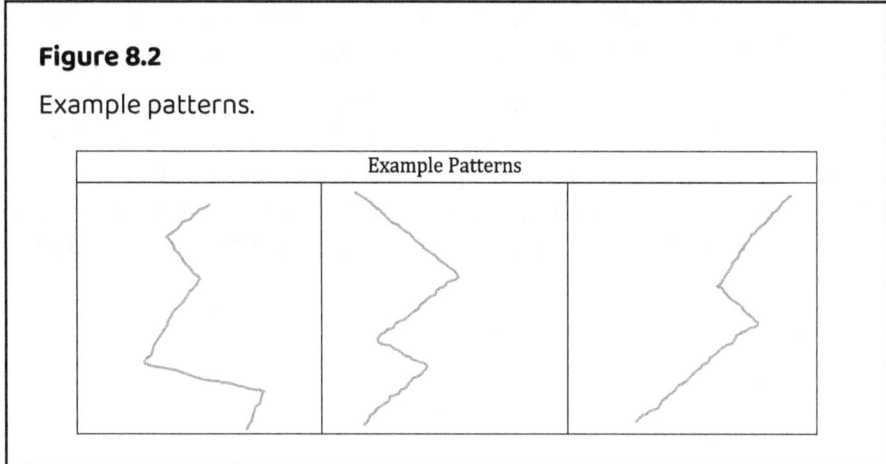

Figure 8.2

Example patterns.

12. Ask the students to imagine that the chip is actually a piece of fossil on a hill in Montana. The same rules apply. Gravity pulls it downward, and it bounces off rocks and plants as it tumbles.
13. Ask a volunteer to recall from the story what the ratio was of meat-eating theropods to plant-eating saurischians and ornithischians (i.e., about 1:20). Explain that is why you only included one theropod at the bottom of the Dino Plinko board.
14. Discuss as a group why this ratio was important to maintain millions of years ago when the dinosaurs were alive (i.e., if there were too many meat eaters, the plant eaters would be killed off and the ecosystem would collapse).
15. Divide students into groups of three or four. Introduce the following problem-based learning scenario:

    Imagine you are a participant signed up to join Saddle Creek's summer dig. You received a welcome packet full of information before your arrival in Montana. Read through the welcome packet and record what you know about your upcoming trip on your Need-to-Know Board.

Dino Plinko

16. Give students the included information packet and a blank *Need-to-Know Board*. Their task is to work as a group to:
    a. Read the information packet and highlight any important statements.
    b. Record what you now know about the dinosaur dig you signed up for in column one of the *Need-to-Know Board*.
    c. Record any questions you would like to ask about the dig in column two.

17. When students have finished, read the following scenario out loud:

    You have been eagerly anticipating the dig for weeks. Day one is finally here. During the morning hours, the paleontologist taught you how to tell the difference between fossilized bone and plain rock, as well as how to follow a bone trail. You are thrilled when you find your first small piece of bone.

18. Ask one person from each group to drop the chip down the Dino Plinko game board and record on their individual *Need-to-Know Boards* whether the chip landed on an ornithischian, saurischian, or theropod. If they do not know, they can use the cladogram used earlier in the unit.

19. Instruct students to complete the following journal prompt:

    If you could find the remains of any dinosaur species, which would you choose and why?

20. Inform the students that they will not be reading a chapter from the novel today.

WELCOME PACKET

Welcome to Saddle Creek's Dino Adventure!

Eric and I are thrilled that you have decided to join us on this epic adventure to uncover the past and discover what has been hidden for millions of years. For the next two weeks, you will learn how to act and think like a paleontologist, while having a lot of fun in the process. All you need to do in order to participate is be willing to listen, get a little dirty, follow the rules outlined in section two, and sign the forms in section three. If you are up to the challenge, please read on.

Rules and Procedures

Because we will be working with fragile fossils that are millions of years old, it is important that you follow all instructions given by the paleontologist. Not doing so may result in the damage or destruction of rare artifacts.

Staying hydrated and keeping your skin protected from the sun is very important. Each participant should drink at least eight glasses of water every day and wear sunscreen at all times.

We will be guests on private land during the dig. All attempts should be made to leave the land as it was before our arrival. This includes properly disposing of garbage, refraining from unnecessary digging, filling in open holes after necessary digging, and not disturbing native plants and animals or cattle owned by the ranchers.

All fossil finds are the property of the paleontologist unless permission is given by the paleontologist for the participant to keep them.

Dino Plinko

Forms and Documents

Initial here once you have read the Antiquities Act of 1906. _____

Initial here if you agree to follow the rules outlined in section two. _____

Initial here if you have faxed or emailed all signed health forms. _____

Initial here if you give permission for photos to be taken during the adventure. _____

Initial here if you agree to *not* hold Saddle Creek Dino Adventures liable in the unlikely event of bodily injury during the next two weeks. _____

Emergency Contact Information

Name of Participant _____

Name of Emergency Contact _____

Relationship to Emergency Contact _____

Phone Number _____

Need-to-Know Board

Name: _____ Date: _____

What We Know	What We Need to Know	Where We Can Find Out	✓
		Assigned to: _____	
		Assigned to: _____	
		Assigned to: _____	
		Assigned to: _____	
		Assigned to: _____	
		Assigned to: _____	
		Assigned to: _____	
		Assigned to: _____	
		Assigned to: _____	
		Assigned to: _____	
		Assigned to: _____	
		Assigned to: _____	
		Assigned to: _____	

Lesson 9

Location Matters

Objectives

- The students will continue exploring the problem-based learning scenario introduced yesterday.
- The students will discuss an ethical situation using De Bono's Thinking Hats.

Materials

- *Need-to-Know Boards*
- Dice
- Student journals

DINOSAURS TO DRONES

Assessments

- Journals
- *Need-to-Know Boards*

Procedures

1. Explain to students that they will *not* be reading a chapter or participating in a choice activity once again today. Instead, they will apply everything they have learned to complete the next phase of the problem-based learning (PBL) task introduced in the previous lesson.

2. Instruct students to arrange themselves into PBL groups and briefly review part one of the scenario (i.e., you joined a dinosaur dig for two weeks, found a piece of dinosaur bone, and began the process of following the bone trail).

3. Introduce part two by asking one person from each PBL group to roll the dice. Explain that the number they roll corresponds to what they "found" after their group followed the bone trail to its source. Display the code below:

   > 1 = Found no other evidence of the skeleton.
   >
   > 2 = Found the entire skeleton, but it is on federal land.
   >
   > 3 = Found the skull of the skeleton only. Roll the dice again. If it lands on an even number, it is on private land. If it lands on an odd number, it is on public land.
   >
   > 4 = Found the entire skeleton and it is on private land.
   >
   > 5 = Found a few shattered remnants, but nothing substantial.
   >
   > 6 = Roll again.

   Note: If a group rolls a number one or five, they can earn another role of the dice by completing one of the following tasks: (a) list three additional locations in the United States where dinosaur fossils are often found, or (b) describe another technique paleontologists use to locate fossils in addition to following the bone trail.

4. Give students time to record this new information on their *Need-to-Know Boards* and then determine as a group what their next steps should be. Students should consider such things as:

    a. What should we do if it is on federal land?

    b. What if the private landowner says we cannot dig any more on their property?

5. Fifteen minutes before class ends, pull the students back together and ask them to record a summary of their proposed next steps in their journals.

6. Find and read a news article like the one below describing someone who broke the law regarding artifacts on public vs. private land: www.cnn.com/2009/TECH/science/03/20/dinosaur.bone.theft.montana/index.html

7. Instruct students to discuss the ethical issues addressed in the article using De Bono's Thinking Hats.

TEACHER NOTE:

For more information on De Bono's Thinking Hats, please refer to the website linked here:

http://www.debonogroup.com/six_thinking_hats.php

8. Ask students to complete the following journal prompt:

    Summarize the discussion the class just had and add any pertinent information to your Need-to-Know Boards.

Lesson 10

Care and Feeding of a Dinosaur

Objectives

- The students will begin researching a dinosaur of their choice.
- The students will critically evaluate a list of next steps created by another group.

Materials

- *Need-to-Know Boards*
- *Grit-O-Meter* chart
- *Care and Feeding of a Dino* handout

DINOSAURS TO DRONES

Assessments

▸ *Need-to-Know Boards*
▸ *Care and Feeding* handout

Procedures

1. Explain to students that they will finish the problem-based learning (PBL) scenario they have been working on today and then continue reading the novel as before.
2. Ask the students to share a few of the tasks they completed yesterday (e.g., determined next steps in their scenario, debated an ethical issue, etc.).
3. Display the *Grit-O-Meter* from lesson two and ask the students to determine the extent to which they have had to use grit to solve this PBL scenario thus far.
4. Instruct each group to share the list of next steps they generated yesterday. After each presentation, open up the floor for those not in the group to ask questions or alert them to potential problems that could lead to breaking the law.
5. Introduce students to the last step in the PBL scenario below:

    Imagine you have been asked by a local museum to create a Care and Feeding *guide for the dinosaur you found in this expedition. Reexamine the cladogram for the branch of the dinosaur family tree your chip landed on. Choose one dinosaur from that branch you would like to become an expert on and then complete the* Care and Feeding of a Dino *handout by yourself or with someone in your PBL group.*

6. Provide the majority of class time for students to work.
7. Five minutes before the class period is over, conduct another whip-around using the sentence stem below:

    My dinosaur is called _____ and three things I have learned about it so far are _____.

8. Collect the completed *Care and Feeding* guides to score and provide feedback on.
9. Read chapter seven of the novel to students, or ask that it be read independently before the next class period.

Name: _____ Date: _____

Care and Feeding of a Dino

Directions: Use the books provided and/or approved websites to research important facts about your chosen dinosaur.

Name of Dinosaur _____

Type of Dinosaur (*circle one*):   Ornithischian   Saurischian   Theropod

---

Primary Food Sources:
_____
_____
_____

Preferred Habitat:
_____
_____
_____

Physical Characteristics:
_____
_____
_____

Labeled Diagram of the Dinosaur: (Draw a picture in the space below)

LESSON 10

Name: _____ Date: _____

More to Explore: (List three unanswered questions you still have about your dinosaur)

1.
2.
3.

Lesson 11

Dreaming Up Drone Duties

Objectives

- The students will explore the physics of drones.
- The students will make predictions regarding how drones will impact our lives in the future.

Materials

- Chapter seven of the book *Dinosaurs, Diggers, and Thieves*
- Timelines
- Drone (if available)

DINOSAURS TO DRONES

- *Continuum of Change* chart
- Student journals

Assessments

- Timelines
- Venn diagrams
- Journal responses

Procedures

1. Review major content introduced during the previous lesson (e.g., physical characteristics, habitat, and major food sources for your chosen dinosaur, etc.).
2. Ask students to work with their groups to add major events from chapter seven of the novel to their timelines.
3. Provide an opportunity for students to share.
4. Take a few minutes for students to share what they know about drones from personal experience.
5. Instruct the students to talk with a partner in order to:
   ▷ Summarize why and how Dorian suggested Sylvia use his drone, and
   ▷ Predict whether or not this would be successful.
6. Explain to students that drones are the perfect example of how quickly technology is advancing. In the early 2000s, drones were simply a novelty and something used only by the military. Their uses have now skyrocketed. Read the statistic below:

   > The US Government made it mandatory for drone hobbyists and businesses using drones to register their drones in December of 2015. As of April 2017 over 770,000 registrations have been processed. That number is expected to triple by 2021. *Kaya Yurieff (April 2017) CNN article "U.S. Drone Registrations Skyrocket"*

Dreaming Up Drone Duties

7. Read to students the excerpt below from the article "Knowledge Doubling Every 12 Months, Soon to be Every 12 Hours" by David Schilling on the website Industrytap.com (2013). Ask the students what surprised them about this.

   > Buckminster Fuller created the "Knowledge Doubling Curve"; he noticed that until 1900 human knowledge doubled approximately every century. By the end of World War II knowledge was doubling every 25 years. Today things are not as simple as different types of knowledge have different rates of growth. For example, nanotechnology knowledge is doubling every two years and clinical knowledge every 18 months. But on average human knowledge is doubling every 13 months. According to IBM, the build out of the "internet of things" will lead to the doubling of knowledge every 12 hours.

8. Ask students to complete a row on their *Continuum of Change* chart regarding the use of drones.

9. Show the students an actual drone and provide a brief tutorial on how to use it.

TEACHER NOTE:

There are many inexpensive drones to choose from if you decide to purchase one for your classroom. I would advise steering clear of the miniature drones, as they are very unstable and unreliable.

10. Poll the students to see if anyone can explain the science behind how drones fly. Based on the degree of student background knowledge, watch a video or read a book similar to the one linked here called the *Basic Physics of Drones*: www.youtube.com/watch?v=PkbkO3e0ev0.

DINOSAURS TO DRONES

11. Provide 20 minutes for students to work on the following choice activities:

CHOICE A	
Materials:	• Student journals
Directions:	Do you know what a horned toad looks like? Look closely at the image shown below (Figure 11.1). How is it different from the typical toad? Scientists recently discovered a new species of dinosaur that resembles a horned toad in many ways. Conduct a search online for the dinosaur known as *Zuul crurivastator*. Create a Venn Diagram or double bubble map comparing a horned toad with the *Zuul crurivastator* in your journal.
Assessment:	You must be able to list three ways in which the two are the same and three ways in which they are different.

Figure 11.1

Horned toad.

Dreaming Up Drone Duties

CHOICE B	
Materials:	• Student journals
Directions:	Brainstorm a list of new innovative ways drones might be used in the future inside your journal. Two creative examples are: a. Drones as plant pollinators – www.cnn.com/2017/05/11/tech/ecosolutions-5-ways-tech/ b. Drones as fashion models on the runway – www.cnn.com/videos/world/2018/06/07/saudi-arabia-fashion-show-drones-lon-orig.cnn/ Choose one possible use from your list and create a T-chart displaying the positives and negatives of this idea in your journal.
Assessment:	You must be able to share the idea you selected and the positives and negatives associated with it.

12. Provide time for each group to share what they discovered.
13. Complete the following journal prompt:

    Imagine the year is 2075. If knowledge doubles every 13 years, about how many times will knowledge have doubled until today? What may the world look like then?

14. Read chapter eight of the novel to students, or ask that it be read independently before the next class period.

Lesson 12

From Bone to Stone

Objectives

- The students will explore how fossils form.
- The students will compare and contrast real bone with fossilized bone.

Materials

- Chapter eight of the book *Dinosaurs, Diggers, and Thieves*
- Raw potato
- Sponge or okra

DINOSAURS TO DRONES

- Stamp pad
- Blank paper
- Cleaned chicken bone
- Real fossil if available (collected by student, purchased online, etc.)
- White, wheat, and rye bread
- Gummy worms or gummy bears
- Heavy books
- Paper towels
- Various books about paleontology
- Timelines
- *Paleontology Lexicon Log*
- Student journals

Assessments

- Timelines
- Journal responses

Procedures

1. Review major content introduced during the previous lesson (e.g., the speed at which knowledge doubles, differences and similarities between horned toads and a new species of dinosaur, how drones fly, etc.).
2. Ask students to work with their groups to add major events from chapter eight of the novel to their timelines.
3. Provide an opportunity for students to share.
4. Explain to students that the incident in this chapter involving Dorian accidentally putting a rabbit bone on his tongue actually happened to the author of this book. The lesson today will focus on determining the difference between fossilized bone, fresh bone, and regular rocks.
5. Cut a potato in half. Place the flat edge of the potato on an ink pad and use it as a stamp on a piece of paper. Explain that this print represents a typical rock one might find while looking for fossils. Now, cut either a sponge or piece of okra in half and repeat the process. This print represents the pattern Dorian is hoping to find.

6. Display the pictures below as well (Figures 12.1 and 12.2):

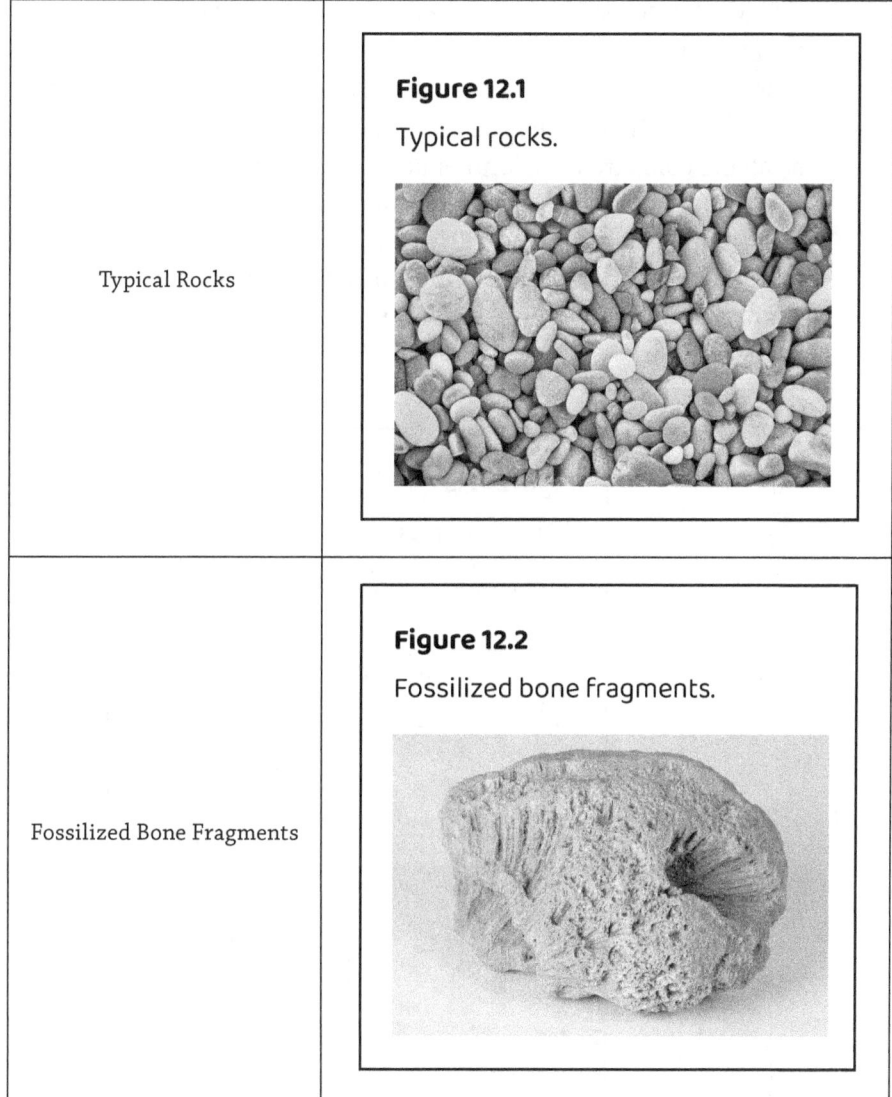

Typical Rocks	**Figure 12.1** Typical rocks.
Fossilized Bone Fragments	**Figure 12.2** Fossilized bone fragments.

7. Ask the students to recall the four key ingredients necessary for a fossil to form Tom listed in chapter three (i.e., water, minerals, time, pressure). Reread this section of the book if necessary.
8. Ask the students to record the four components above on their *Paleontology Lexicon Log* next to the words *Ingredients for Fossilization*.
9. Show a video or read a nonfiction text about the fossilization process similar to the example included here called "How do dinosaur fossils form?": https://www.youtube.com/watch?v=87E8bQrX4Wg:

10. Reiterate the fact that fossilized bones are actually no longer bones at all. This is because the bone was slowly replaced with minerals over time. Once the minerals harden, a new rock is produced in the shape of the bone.
11. Ask students to examine a chicken bone and compare it to a fossilized bone. If possible, use real bones and fossils. If not, have the students compare the pictures below (Figures 12.3 and 12.4). Ask the students to use their senses (or imagination if using pictures only) to list similarities and differences of the two bones (e.g., fossil is heavier than the chicken bone, both differ in color, one is harder than the other).

Figure 12.3

Chicken bones.

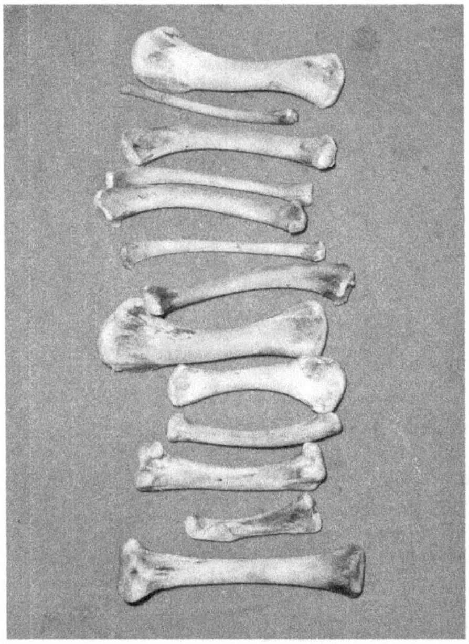

Chicken Bone

From Bone to Stone

Fossilized Bone	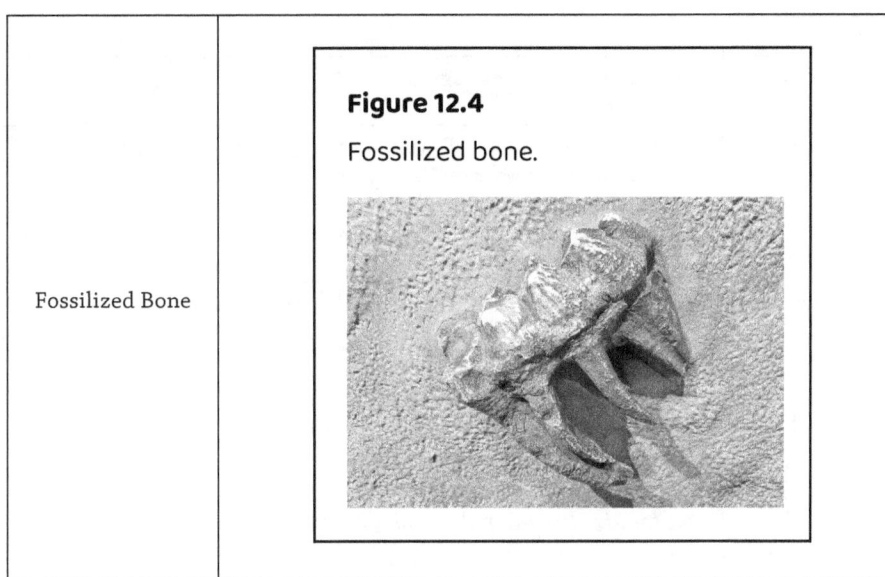**Figure 12.4** Fossilized bone.

12. Provide 20 minutes for students to work on one of the following choice activities:

CHOICE A	
Materials:	- One piece of white bread - One piece of wheat bread - One piece of rye bread - Several gummy worms or gummy bears - Two paper towels - Three or four heavy books - Student journal
Directions:	Place a paper towel on the table. Stack two pieces of bread on top of the paper towel. Place gummy worms or bears on the bread. Add the last piece of bread and then the second paper towel. Put the heavy books on top of the paper towel. Predict what you think the combination of bread and gummy candies will look like in 24 hours. In your journal, write a paragraph describing how this might be similar to how fossils form.

Assessment:	You must be able to:
	  a. Explain what you constructed, and
	  b. Share the paragraph you wrote

DINOSAURS TO DRONES

CHOICE B	
Materials:	• Books about paleontology • Student journal
Directions:	At the end of the chapter, Dorian is eagerly awaiting the next day, when he will get to work on Victoria with Tom. Search through the books provided or online to create a list of five tips new paleontologists need to know when working with an actual fossilized dinosaur specimen. Record these tips in your journal.
Assessment:	You must be able to share your list of five tips and the sources you used to create it.

13. Provide time for each group to share what they discovered.

14. Answer the following journal prompt:

    If you could ask a real paleontologist anything, what would it be?

15. Read chapter nine of the novel to students, or ask that it be read independently before the next class period.

Lesson 13

Dynamic Deductions

Objectives

- The students will practice using and creating if-then statements.
- The students will create the converse and inverse of if-then statements.

Materials

- Chapter nine of the book *Dinosaurs, Diggers, and Thieves*
- Whiteboard or chart paper
- Timelines
- Student journals

DINOSAURS TO DRONES

Assessments

- Timelines
- Journal responses

Procedures

1. Review major content introduced during the previous lesson (e.g., how to tell the difference between a normal stone and a fossil, tips for beginner paleontologists, etc.)
2. Ask students to work with their groups to add major events from chapter nine of the novel to their timelines.
3. Provide an opportunity for students to share.
4. Ask the students the following question: "What coding concept did Dorian use to help him deduce that the thieves might return?" (i.e., the *if-then statement*)
5. Explain that according to the Java tutorial created by Oracle, "The if-then statement is the most basic of all the control flow statements. It tells your program to execute a certain section of code *only if* a particular test evaluates to true." (Found at https://docs.oracle.com/javase/tutorial/java/nutsandbolts/if.html.)
6. Explain that an example of an if-then statement Dorian might have generated is:

    If the entire skeleton is more valuable than a partial skeleton, **then** the thieves may return to steal the rest of the skeleton.

7. Provide the following two examples from the real world:
    a. **If** smoke is detected, **then** turn on the fire sprinkler inside the building,
    b. **If** it rains, **then** it will be wet.
8. Ask each student to create three of their own if-then condition statements from observations they have made in the real world. Give students an opportunity to share at least one with the whole class.
9. Explain that what we have just done is use *deductive logic*. Deductive logic is the process of using a few statements to come to a relatively certain conclusion about something. When using deductive logic, one answer is deemed the correct answer.

10. Introduce the terms *converse* and *inverse* by writing the following on the board:
    a. The converse of **if** A, **then** B would be **if** B, **then** A.
    b. The inverse of **if** A, **then** B would be **if** NOT A, **then** NOT B.
11. Ask the students to reexamine the three if-then statements they originally created. Challenge them to generate and record in their journals the converse and inverse of each.
12. Instruct students to trade journals with someone else. Their task is to determine if the converse and inverse statements generated by the other person are written correctly and if they are true (i.e., whether they would actually happen in the real world). For example, the converse of example A in step seven above is true (i.e., if the fire sprinkler is on, then smoke was detected in the building). On the other hand, the converse of example B is not necessarily true (i.e., if it's wet, then it rained). There could be many other explanations for why it is wet outside.
13. Challenge the class as a whole to generate examples of how knowing how to generate if-then statements, as well as their converse and inverse, might be beneficial.
14. Provide 20 minutes for students to work on one of the following choice activities:

CHOICE A	
Materials:	• Student journal
Directions:	Conduct a search online to find websites specializing in deductive logic puzzles. Example websites include: • https://brainbashers.com/logic.asp • www.briddles.com/riddles/deductive-reasoning Solve two or three on your own and then work with a partner to create a new deductive logic puzzle. Record this in your journal.
Assessment:	You must be able to share the logic puzzle you created.

CHOICE B	
Materials:	• Student journal
Directions:	Go to Code.org online and create your own account using the STUDENT option. Begin the course appropriate for your grade level. After 15–20 minutes of exploration, write a summary of what you learned in your journal. In the future, you may work on Code.org at home or when you finish an assignment early in class after obtaining permission from the teacher.
Assessment:	You must be able to explain what you learned and why you think coding is important to learn.

TEACHER NOTE:

Code.org has many wonderful free resources for teachers as well. Not all of the lessons involve actual coding on a computer either. Consider checking out and using the "Unplugged" lessons they provide at the following website:

https://code.org/curriculum/unplugged

15. Provide time for each group to share what they discovered.
16. Complete the following journal prompt:

    Please write the converse and inverse of the if-then statement that follows:

    IF I WORK HARD, **THEN** MY EFFORTS WILL PAY OFF.

17. Read chapter ten of the novel to students, or ask that it be read independently before the next class period.

Lesson 14

Deciphering a Dinosaur Dilemma

Objectives

- The students will use deductive logic to make inferences using events from the past.
- The students will investigate constellations visible in Montana during different parts of the year.

Materials

- Chapter ten of the book *Dinosaurs, Diggers, and Thieves*
- *Deciphering a Dinosaur Dilemma* worksheet
- Timelines
- Student journals

DINOSAURS TO DRONES

Assessments

- Timelines
- *Deciphering a Dinosaur Dilemma* responses
- Journal responses

Procedures

1. Review major content introduced during the previous lesson (e.g., how to write and understand if-then statements, coding concepts uncovered from exploring Code.org, etc.).
2. Ask students to work with their groups to add major events from chapter ten of the novel to their timelines.
3. Provide an opportunity for students to share.
4. Ask the students to discuss with a partner how Dorian and Eric used deductive logic in the chapter (e.g., determining the hours when the theft most likely occurred and how many people were involved, etc.).
5. Distribute a copy of the *Deciphering a Dinosaur Dilemma* worksheet to each student. Ask students to imagine they are paleontologists and come across the fossilized footprints pictured (see Figure 14.1). Instruct students to analyze them carefully, infer what they think happened to create them, and write their response in the appropriate spot. (Note: One possible explanation is that the large dinosaur is a theropod and it attacked a plant-eating saurischian or ornithischian. The line between the footsteps was made by the tail. It was dragging until it saw the plant-eater and began to run. Most likely, there was a plant or small hill blocking their view of each other until the last minute.)
6. Ask the students to create their own dinosaur footprint puzzle on the back of the handout. When they are finished, students should challenge a partner to interpret what they think took place. The partner doing the guessing can ask *yes* or *no* questions to help generate the solution.
7. Remind students that in this chapter, we learn about Dorian's interest in astronomy. Ask the students to generate a list of everything they know about astronomy on the board as a group.

8. Provide 20 minutes for students to work on the choice activities below:

CHOICE A	
Materials:	• Books about constellations • Student journals
Directions:	In this chapter, Dorian and Eric saw the constellation Orion in the sky. Assuming the story takes place in June or July, what are five other constellations visible in the Montana sky during that time of year? Draw and label a pictorial diagram of each in your journal. One good place to start is the website for the Southwest Montana Astronomical Society, found at https://smasweb.org.
Assessment:	You must be able to share your list of constellations and the accompanying diagrams.

CHOICE B	
Materials:	• Books about wildlife in Montana • Student journal
Directions:	You now know that coyotes, rattlesnakes, and horned toads can be found in Montana. Use the provided books, as well as the internet, to generate a list of other interesting plants and animals Dorian might encounter during his year on the ranch inside your journal. After your list reaches 15 to 20 plants and animals, categorize them into groups according to criteria that make sense to you (e.g., helpful plants, dangerous animals, etc.). If time permits, choose the plant or animal you know the least about and read about it in depth.
Assessment:	You must be able to share your list of plants and animals, as well as how you organized them.

9. Provide time for each group to share what they discovered.
10. Respond to the following journal prompt:

    What other branches of science can you name besides astronomy and paleontology?

11. Read chapter eleven of the novel to students, or ask that it be read independently before the next class period.

Name: _____ Date: _____

Deciphering a Dinosaur Dilemma

Directions: Imagine you came across the following fossilized footprints embedded in rock (Figure 14.1). Look at them carefully and describe what you think occurred here over 65 million years ago.

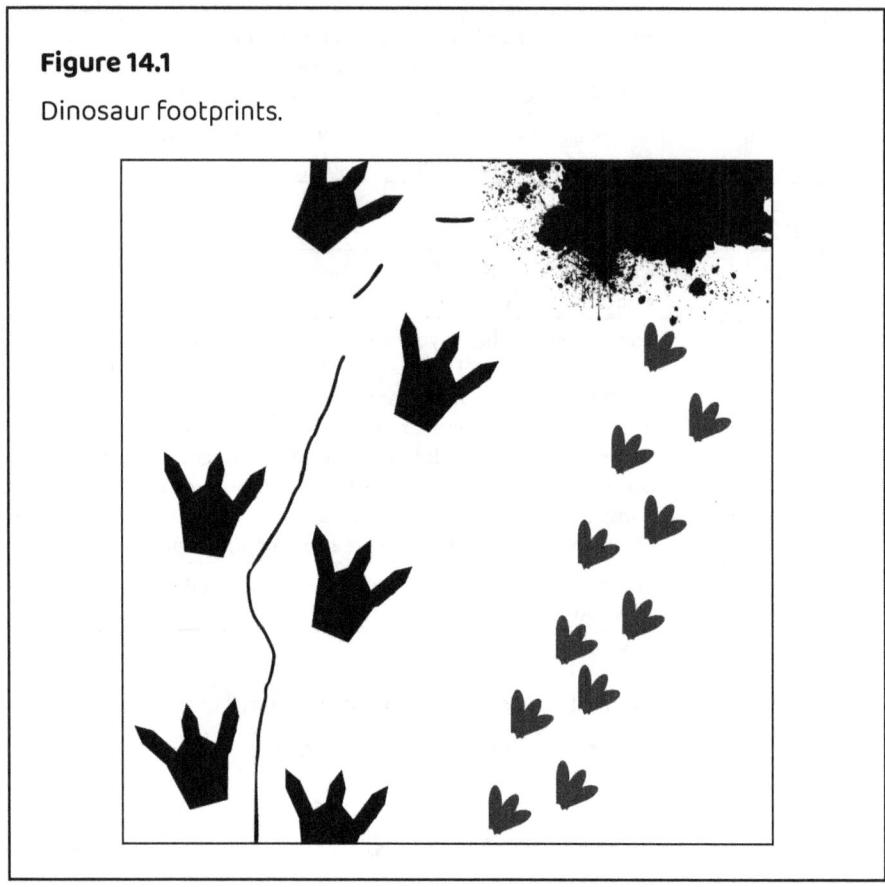

Figure 14.1
Dinosaur footprints.

Your Inferences:

Turn this paper over and create your own dinosaur footprint sketch.

Lesson 15

Fighting Fears and Considering Cycles

Objectives

- The students will differentiate between rational and irrational fears.
- The students will create a model of two cycles in nature (i.e., a rock cycle and phases of the moon).

Materials

- Chapter eleven of the book *Dinosaurs, Diggers, and Thieves*
- Timelines
- *Grit-O-Meter*

DINOSAURS TO DRONES

- *Continuum of Change* chart
- Flashlight
- Ball
- *Earthsteps: A Rock's Journey through Time* by Diane Nelson Spickert
- Student journals

Assessments

- Demonstration of phases of the moon
- Timelines
- Journal responses

Procedures

1. Review major content introduced during the previous lesson (e.g., how to infer from dinosaur footprints, constellations visible in Montana, etc.).
2. Ask students to work with their groups to add major events from chapter eleven of the novel to their timelines.
3. Provide an opportunity for students to share.
4. Remind students that Dorian experienced a very scary situation in chapter eleven. Ask the students to think about a time when they were truly scared. Give students an opportunity to share how their bodies reacted to the scary situation. Did your heart rate speed up? Did your palms get sweaty?
5. Explain that sometimes people choose to head into danger instead of away (e.g., a firefighter rescuing someone in a burning building). Ask the students what motivated Dorian and Eric to head toward potential danger in this chapter.
6. Create a T-chart on the board with *rational fears* on one side and *irrational fears* on the other. Ask the students to discuss with a partner what the words rational and irrational mean.
7. Define *rational fear* as "something that could potentially happen" and *irrational fear* as "something that most likely would not." Examples of rational fears include (a) someone breaking into your home when you are away, or (b) getting into a car crash when the

roads are wet. Examples of irrational fears include being afraid of (a) getting into a swimming pool because of a fear of sharks, or (b) a monster living under your bed.

8. Challenge students to brainstorm in small groups three or four additional rational and irrational fears.

9. When students have finished, ask why it is important to distinguish between the two types of fears (e.g., knowing irrational fears are unlikely to happen can relieve stress and anxiety).

TEACHER NOTE:

If your students tend to worry about the things they cannot control, consider providing the book *What to Do When You Worry Too Much* by Dawn Huebner. This book is a part of a series of books written for kids to help them with social/emotional problems such as perfectionism, anger, dealing with obsessive-compulsive disorder, etc.

10. Provide 20 minutes for students to work on the choice activities below:

CHOICE A	
Materials:	• *Earthsteps: A Rock's Journey through Time* by Diane Nelson Spickert • *Grit-O-Meter* • *Continuum of Change* chart • Student journal
Directions:	In this chapter, Eric hurt his ankle by falling into a rain rut. Rain ruts form as a result of erosion. Read the book *Earthsteps: A Rock's Journey through Time* and describe the rock cycle it explains in your journal. Next, using your *Grit-O-Meter*, rate the amount of grit it takes to turn a boulder into a grain of sand. Finally, complete a row on your *Continuum of Change* chart for this boulder. If time permits, research erosion further online.

Assessment:	You must be able to:
	    a. Describe the rock cycle, and
	    b. Share your *Grit-O-Meter* rating

CHOICE B	
Materials:	- Flashlight - Ball - Student journal
Directions:	Several times in this chapter the characters lamented the fact that there was no moon to light their way. Research the phases of the moon using the nonfiction texts provided and the internet. Make sure to draw a diagram of the phases of the moon in your journal. Once you understand how and why the moon changes throughout the month, use a flashlight and a ball to model the phases of the moon with a friend.

Assessment:	You must be able to:
	  a. Describe the phases of the moon, and
	  b. Demonstrate the phases of the moon using a ball and flashlight

11. Provide time for each group to share what they discovered.
12. Complete the following journal prompt:

    My biggest fear is...because...

13. Read chapter twelve of the novel to students, or ask that it be read independently before the next class period.

Lesson 16

Reexamining Relationships

Objectives

- The students will research the five types of foreshadowing used in literature.
- The students will apply the concept of change to relationships between people.

Materials

- Chapter twelve of the book *Dinosaurs, Diggers, and Thieves*
- Timelines
- *Continuum of Change* chart
- Student journals

DINOSAURS TO DRONES

Assessments

- Journal responses
- Timelines

Procedures

1. Review major content introduced during the previous lesson (e.g., rational vs. irrational fears, the rock cycle, phases of the moon, etc.).
2. Ask students to work with their groups to add major events from chapter twelve of the novel to their timelines.
3. Provide an opportunity for students to share.
4. Poll the students to see how many were surprised by the explanation Susan gave for not telling Dorian about Great-Uncle Philip for so long.
5. Point out that Dorian used the word *anticlimactic* to describe his thoughts about his mother's story. Ask the students to use context clues or previous knowledge to decode the meaning of this word. Define anticlimactic as "not as exciting as expected."
6. Remind students that relationships undergo change just like rocks do over the decades and the moon does each month. One way that this happens is when people learn from their or someone else's mistakes and attempt not to repeat them. Ask the students to find an example of this in chapter twelve (e.g., Susan doesn't want to repeat the mistake her mother made regarding not talking about her feelings).
7. Instruct students to identify a relationship in their own lives that has changed (e.g., a friend moved away, a grandparent passed away, etc.), then record and rate this change on their *Continuum of Change* chart.
8. Debate the following questions in small groups or together as a class:

    Imagine you are Susan and you just received the letter from your Uncle Philip a week or two after your mother's passing. Would you have written back? If so, what would you have said? If not, why not?

Reexamining Relationships

9. Provide 20 minutes for students to work on the choice activities below:

CHOICE A	
Materials:	• Student journal
Directions:	At the end of this chapter, Dorian reveals he has an idea for capturing the thieves and retrieving the skeleton. Think about clues in previous chapters that might help us determine what Dorian's plan might include. Pay special attention to chapter eleven. Record your theory in your journal, and then research the five types of foreshadowing online or in a grammar book. Finally, answer the question below in your journal: In your opinion, which type of foreshadowing did the author use at the conclusion of chapter eleven?
Assessment:	You must be able to: a. Share your theory about what Dorian's idea could include, b. List the five types of foreshadowing, and c. Identify how you classified the foreshadowing used in chapter eleven

CHOICE B	
Materials:	• Student journal
Directions:	Have you ever been concentrating on something so completely that time seemed to melt away? Hours go by and it seems like just a few minutes? Psychologists refer to this as finding *flow*. Reflect on chapter twelve and find an example of when Dorian was in flow. What helps you achieve flow? Is it drawing, reading, video games, etc.? Write the definition of flow and how you achieve it in your journal. Next, spend time engaging in your flow activity after getting permission from the teacher.
Assessment:	You must be able to: a. Describe what flow is, and b. Give examples from your own life

10. Provide time for each group to share what they discovered.
11. Complete the following journal prompt:

TEACHER NOTE:

According to Rick Miller, the founder of Kids at Hope, one of the things that creates hope in students is the ability to envision their future. Tomorrow, they will have an opportunity to begin thinking about the career they might like to pursue. Another way for them to envision their future is to think about the hobbies and leisure activities they would like to participate in as an adult. Consider tying this idea with the concept of flow by asking, "How would you like to experience flow when you are an adult?"

Which of the following people do you think will be willing to help Dorian and Eric: Sylvia, Jose, or Zade? Why or why not?

12. Read chapter thirteen of the novel to students, or ask that it be read independently before the next class period.

Lesson 17

Creatures and Careers

Objectives

▶ The students will determine what educational background and experience are necessary for someone to become a practicing paleontologist.

▶ The students will research one or more of the fictional creatures mentioned by Jose.

Materials

▶ Chapter thirteen of the book *Dinosaurs, Diggers, and Thieves*
▶ Timelines

- *Grit-O-Meter*
- *Continuum of Change* chart
- Student journals

Assessments

- Journal responses
- Timelines

Procedures

1. Review major content introduced during the previous lesson (e.g., the mystery surrounding Uncle Philip, types of foreshadowing, the concept of flow, etc.).
2. Ask students to work with their groups to add major events from chapter thirteen of the novel to their timelines.
3. Provide an opportunity for students to share.
4. Ask the students to define the terms *extrovert* and *introvert*. Next, challenge students to classify Zade and Jose into each of these categories (i.e., Zade is an introvert, Jose is an extrovert). After hearing students' classifications, ask for evidence from the story that explains their thinking.
5. Ask students to complete an introvert/extrovert scale similar to the one linked here: http://fortune.com/2015/06/03/cain-introvert-quiz/.
6. Poll the students to determine if anyone was surprised by his or her results.
7. Ask the students to discuss whether or not they think a personality trait like being an extrovert or an introvert can change over time. Why or why not?

Creatures and Careers

8. Provide 20 minutes for students to work on the choice activities below:

CHOICE A	
Materials:	- *Grit-O-Meter* - Student journal
Directions:	In this chapter, Zade reveals that he would like to become a paleontologist. Research which universities offer a program leading to a degree in paleontology, what the degree requirements are, and about how much money he will need to raise. Record this information in your journal. Next, look for job openings in the paleontological field and determine what salary Zade could expect to earn once he graduates from college. Lastly, predict how much grit you believe it would take someone to complete all of these requirements.

Assessment:	You must be able to:
	    a. List three or four universities that have paleontology programs,
	    b. Share what it takes to become a paleontologist, and
	    c. Provide a typical salary for a paleontologist

CHOICE B	
Materials:	- *Continuum of Change* chart - Student journal

Directions:	Your task is to compare and contrast three of the creatures mentioned by Jose in this chapter using a Venn diagram. Draw and complete your three-ring Venn diagram in your journal. You may choose from:
	    - Thunderbirds
	    - Kraken
	    - Sirrush
	    - Ogopogo
	    - Mokele-mbembe
	Next, talk with a partner about what the implications would be if the creatures you chose to compare were real and alive today. Rate the level of change it would require from us using the *Continuum of Change* chart.

Assessment:	You must be able to:
	    a. Describe the differences and similarities of the creatures you compared, and
	    b. Share you prediction as to how life would change if these creatures were proven to exist

DINOSAURS TO DRONES

9. Provide time for each group to share what they discovered.

10. Because the journal prompt today will require completing a little bit of research first, provide additional time for students to work. Ask the students to complete the following journal prompt:

    Today many of you explored what it takes to become a paleontologist. Now, think about what you would like to be when you grow up. Research and record the type of training you will need to complete in order to make this a reality. If time permits, record the average salary for someone with this career and two or more colleges that offer this program.

11. Read chapter fourteen of the novel to students, or ask that it be read independently before the next class period.

Lesson 18

Predator Competitors

Objectives

- The students will read about and compare ancient apex predators and modern-day apex predators.
- The students will choose one of the habits of highly organized people and create a plan for incorporating it into their lives.

Materials

- Chapter fourteen of the book *Dinosaurs, Diggers, and Thieves*
- Timelines

- *Apex Predators: The World's Deadliest Hunters, Past and Present* by Steve Jenkins
- *Predator Competitor TKO* handout
- Dice
- *Continuum of Change* chart
- *Paleontology Lexicon Log*
- Student journals

Assessments

- Journal responses
- Timelines
- *Continuum of Change* chart
- *Predator Competitor TKO* handout

Procedures

1. Review major content introduced during the previous lesson (e.g., introvert vs. extrovert, characteristics of various cryptozoology creatures, how to become a paleontologist, etc.).
2. Ask students to work with their groups to add major events from chapter fourteen of the novel to their timelines.
3. Provide an opportunity for students to share.
4. Reread the last line of paragraph one in chapter fourteen. Ask the students if they have ever seen or used a rotary dial phone. (Optional: Show the following video clip of kids reacting to an old phone: www.youtube.com/watch?v=XkuirEweZvM.)
5. Instruct students to complete an entry on their *Continuum of Change* chart regarding the invention of modern smartphones.
6. Discuss the meaning of the phrase "rumor mill." Next, play the old game *Telephone* to demonstrate how rumors can spread quickly and become misconstrued (i.e., whisper a sentence into one student's ear and ask them to pass it to the next person until every student has had a turn. Ask the last person to say what they heard and compare it to the original.)

Predator Competitors

7. Provide 20 minutes for students to work on the choice activities below:

CHOICE A	
Materials:	- *Apex Predators: The World's Deadliest Hunters, Past and Present* - *Predator Competitor TKO* handout - Dice - *Paleontology Lexicon Log*
Directions:	One component of Dorian and Eric's plan is to spread a rumor that a new theropod species of dinosaur has been found. Theropods were the apex predators of their day. Read the book *Apex Predators* by Steve Jenkins. After reading the book, define the term *apex predator* on your *Paleontology Lexicon* page. Finally, follow the directions on the *Predator Competitor TKO* handout with a partner to determine which of various predators would win in a matchup.
Assessment:	You must be able to: a. Assist those who did not choose this activity define apex predator on their *Paleontology Lexicon Log*, and b. Demonstrate how to play the *Predator Competitor TKO* game

CHOICE B	
Materials:	- Student journal
Directions:	The plan Dorian and Eric are concocting is quite complex. It is going to require that they stay extremely organized and communicate well with the other diggers. Well-organized people keep things simple, develop routines, keep a to-do list, have a place for everything, toss clutter daily, and avoid perfectionism when possible. Research the six habits of highly effective people online and define them in your journal. Next, choose one of the six habits you would like to improve. Create a plan for how you will incorporate this into your life. If time permits, get a jump start by practicing your habit until the end of class.
Assessment:	You must be able to: a. Share the six habits of highly effective people, and b. Share how you plan to improve in one of those areas in the future

TEACHER NOTE:

There is a growing body of literature addressing executive functioning in students. Here are a few to explore:

Self-regulation in the Classroom by Richard Cash

How the Gifted Brain Learns by David Sousa

No Mind Left Behind: Understanding and Fostering Executive Control by Adam Cox

8. Provide time for each group to share what they discovered.
9. Complete the following journal prompt:

    What do you think the second phase of Eric and Dorian's plan will entail?

10. Read chapter fifteen of the novel to students or ask that it be read independently before the next class period.

Name: _____ Date: _____

Predator Competitor TKO

Directions: The acronym TKO stands for *technical knockout* in the world of competitive boxing. Imagine you and your partner are competitors in the boxing ring. This is a two-player game so the first step is to find a partner. Next, each player should roll the dice. The number rolled corresponds to the options you have to choose from in each round. Your choice should be kept a secret and recorded in the space provided at the bottom of this page. When both of you are ready, reveal your selections at the same time. Next, use the book *Apex Predators* by Steve Jenkins to determine which apex predator would win that round of the fight. Make sure to pay attention to whether the fight is on land, air, or water. The person with the most points after 12 rounds is the winner and earns the TKO!

Apex Predators

	Choice 1	*Choice 2*	*Choice 3*
⚀	Terror Bird	Saber-Tooth Tiger	Giant Freshwater Ray
⚁	Komodo Dragon	Teratorn	Titanoboa
⚂	Mosasaurs	Dimetrodon	Utahraptor
⚃	Anomalocaris	African Wild Dogs	Daeodon
⚄	Dunkleosteus	Giant Short-Faced Bear	Great White Shark
⚅	Hatzegopteryx	Fossa	Siberian Tiger

LESSON 18

109

LESSON 18

The Boxing Ring

Round #	Setting	My Choice	Partner's Choice	1 Point if You Won	Round #	Setting	My Choice	Partner's Choice	1 Point if You Won
1	Land				7	Sea			
2	Air				8	Land			
3	Sea				9	Land			
4	Land				10	Sea			
5	Land				11	Air			
6	Sea				12	Land			

Lesson 19

Hand-Drawing a Hadrosaur

Objectives

- The students will follow the steps paleontologists use to sketch dinosaur fossils out in the field.
- The students will learn how GPS works and how it has impacted our lives.

Materials

- Chapter fifteen of the book *Dinosaurs, Diggers, and Thieves*
- Timelines
- Pictures A, B, and C (Figures 19.1–19.3)

DINOSAURS TO DRONES

- Modified graph paper (attached)
- *Continuum of Change* chart
- Student journals

Assessments

- Journal responses
- Timelines
- *Continuum of Change* chart
- Student sketches

Procedures

1. Review major content introduced during the previous lesson (e.g., apex predators, habits of highly effective people, etc.).
2. Ask students to work with their groups to add major events from chapter fifteen of the novel to their timelines.
3. Provide an opportunity for students to share.
4. Remind students that Dorian used GPS to mark the location of the fossil. Ask the students to talk with a partner about what they know about GPS. Show a video or article about the development of the global positioning system. An example video is linked here: www.youtube.com/watch?v=6JcNb9VhpxI.
5. Ask students to record the consequences of the invention of GPS on their *Continuum of Change* chart.

6. Provide 20 minutes for students to work on the choice activities below:

CHOICE A	
Materials:	<ul><li>Printed pictures A and B</li><li>Modified graph paper</li><li>Projection of picture C onto a wall or screen</li></ul>
Directions:	Before moving a fossil, a practicing paleontologist needs to take photos, draw sketches, use a Brunton, etc. Obviously, in this chapter, Dorian did not have time to follow the normal protocols. One way paleontologists and archaeologists document their finds is to sketch the objects using a grid. A grid breaks a large area or object into smaller pieces. Examine the two pictures of the dinosaur being drawn using a grid. Picture A shows the skeleton with the grid lying against the wall of the dig site (lower left corner). Picture B shows the result. Use the modified graph paper your teacher will give you to recreate the picture your teacher will project onto the screen. When you are finished, talk with a partner about why paleontologists go through the trouble of sketching specimens.
Assessment:	You must be able to describe the process you went through to sketch the dinosaur and why you think paleontologists do this.

Figure 19.1

Picture A.

DINOSAURS TO DRONES

Figure 19.2
Picture B.

Figure 19.3
Picture C.

Hand-Drawing a Hadrosaur

CHOICE B	
Materials:	• Student journal
Directions:	Answer the following questions in your journal: a. Did Dorian break the Antiquities Act by moving the fossil he found on federal land? Why or why not? b. How could Dorian explain to his parents where he was and why he was late without telling a lie? c. What do you think the odds are that someone would find a piece of dinosaur bone as quickly as Dorian did in this chapter? When you are finished, discuss your answers with a partner or in a small group. Where did you and your partner agree?
Assessment:	You must be able to: a. Answer the question stated above, and b. Discuss your thinking with a partner

7. Provide time for each group to share what they discovered.
8. Complete the following journal prompt:

    Dorian was under a lot of stress during this chapter. Write about a time when you felt pressure to complete a task with a quickly approaching deadline.

9. Read chapter sixteen of the novel to students, or ask that it be read independently before the next class period.

Modified Graph Paper

Lesson 20

Profile on Prejudice

Objectives

- The students will analyze a detailed plan and use deductive logic to discover potential flaws.
- The students will discuss the meaning of *prejudice* and why it occurs.

Materials

- Chapter sixteen of the book *Dinosaurs, Diggers, and Thieves*
- Timelines
- *How Drones Work* by Baby Professor
- Student journals

Assessments

▶ Journal responses
▶ Timelines

Procedures

1. Review major content introduced during the previous lesson (e.g., using a grid to create accurate drawings of fossil specimens, how GPS works, etc.).
2. Ask students to work with their groups to add major events from chapter sixteen of the novel to their timelines.
3. Provide an opportunity for students to share.
4. Ask the students to talk with a partner to define the word *prejudice*. Provide an opportunity for groups to share what they came up with and then read the definition below taken from the *Oxford English Dictionary*: "Preconceived opinion that is not based on reason or actual experience."
5. Challenge the students to find two examples from chapter sixteen where Zade might have experienced a form of prejudice (i.e., walking into Martha's on Main and Cassandra treating him as inferior because her father gave him a scholarship). Next, ask the students to brainstorm reasons why those situations might have occurred.
6. Divide students into small groups and give each one of the scenarios found in the table below. Ask each group to compare the scenario they were given to Zade's experiences and determine how they would handle it if it happened to them.

Real-Life Scenarios	
• You are a recent immigrant from Mexico and your family just moved to a small town in Ohio. You are the only Hispanic student in your class and no one talked to you at lunch or recess.	• You are one of two girls in an advanced math class. After you make a careless mistake, one of your classmates leans over and says, "That's okay. Girls aren't supposed to be good at math anyway."
• You are an American citizen of Arabic descent. While walking to the park with your family, you notice a non-Arabic family crossing the street to avoid you.	• You are Jewish and do not celebrate Christmas. Your class has a Christmas party planned and the music teacher has asked everyone to sing "Silent Night" and "We Three Kings" at a concert.

Profile on Prejudice

7. Provide 20 minutes for students to work on the choice activities below:

CHOICE A	
Materials:	• Paper copy of chapter 16 • Student journal
Directions:	In this chapter, Dorian and Eric lay out the next phase of their plan for their friends. Please complete the two tasks below and record your answers in your journal: a. Reread chapter 16 and use deductive logic in the form of if-then statements to determine where something might go wrong. b. Predict what Dorian's role might be in the master plan. If time permits, devise a solution for several of the flaws you identify in part A above.
Assessment:	You must be able to: a. Share your if-then statements, and b. Share your prediction about Dorian's possible role

CHOICE B	
Materials:	• The book *How Drones Work* by Baby Professor
Directions:	Spoiler Alert— *A drone will play a part in the remaining phases of the master plan.* We discussed how drones work earlier in this unit. To refresh your memory, read the book *How Drones Work*. Despite the differences between a drone and an airplane, the same four forces of flight keep them airborne. Conduct research online or use the books provided to discover what the four forces of flight are. List them as well as their definitons in your journal.
Assessment:	You must be able to define the four forces of flight and help those who did not choose this activity understand them as well.

8. Provide time for each group to share what they discovered.
9. Complete the following journal prompt:

    Write about a time when someone had a preconceived opinion of you.

10. Read chapter seventeen of the novel to students, or ask that it be read independently before the next class period.

Lesson 21

Designing a Drone

Objectives

- The students will analyze a story and identify numerous examples when the main characters showed grit.
- The students will build a model of the four propellers on a quadcopter.

Materials

- Chapter seventeen of the book *Dinosaurs, Diggers, and Thieves*
- Timelines
- One 12-inch by 12-inch square of corrugated cardboard per person

DINOSAURS TO DRONES

- Scissors
- Glue
- Compass (the type used to draw circles)
- Ruler
- Student journals

Assessments

- Journal responses
- Timelines
- Student-created models

Procedures

1. Review major content introduced during the previous lesson (e.g., the four forces of flight, the definition of prejudice, etc.).
2. Ask students to work with their groups to add major events from chapter seventeen of the novel to their timelines.
3. Provide an opportunity for students to share.
4. Ask students to recall the definition of the word *grit* (e.g., to be persistent, not give up, and keep on going no matter what).
5. Challenge students to work with a partner to list at least five times Dorian and Eric displayed grit in the novel so far. If students need an example, remind them how Dorian did not give up when he found out Cassandra forgot her camera. Instead, he decided to use his drone.
6. After each pair of students has shared one example from the story, ask volunteers to share examples from their own lives.
7. Read each of the choice activities aloud and allow the students to choose. Explain to students that if they choose option A, they must choose option A tomorrow as well. Conversely, if they do not choose option A, they cannot choose option A tomorrow. Write these requirements as if-then statements.

Designing a Drone

CHOICE A	
Materials:	<ul><li>One 12-inch by 12-inch square of corrugated cardboard per person</li><li>Scissors</li><li>Glue</li><li>Compass (the type used to draw circles)</li><li>Ruler</li></ul>
Directions:	In this chapter, Dorian was forced to use his drone instead of Cassandra's camera. Today you will build a model of the four propellers on a quadcopter similar to Dorian's. Tomorrow you will use your model to demonstrate the four forces of flight. a. Measure and cut out a ¼-inch by 8-inch strip of cardboard. It is important that you measure and cut across the ridges instead of between them. Repeat until you have four strips in total (see Figure 21.1 below). **Figure 21.1** Cardboard strips. b. Draw and cut out four circles 2 inches in diameter using the compass.

123

DINOSAURS TO DRONES

	c. Glue one strip of cardboard to the outside edge of each circle so that the ridges face outward (see Figure 21.2 below). **Figure 21.2** Cardboard propellers. *Final product (Part 1)* d. Cut a 6-inch by 6-inch base from the remaining cardboard (see above, in Figure 21.2). e. Set the pieces aside to dry until tomorrow If you finish early, read the information on the following website: https://uavcoach.com/how-to-fly-a-quadcopter-guide/.
Assessment:	You must be able to share the process you went through to create your four propellers.

CHOICE B	
Materials:	• Books on astronomy or the internet • Student Journal
Directions:	The diggers used the excuse of stargazing to stay up late and be on the ranch when the thieves might attempt to return. In this chapter, Dorian pretended to try to convince Jose to stay with the group by promising to point out the closest stars to Earth. Conduct research and create a list in your journal of the 26 stars that are closest to us. Next, answer the question below: How much farther is the 26th star from Earth than the closest star? Write the answer in the form of a ratio.
Assessment:	You must be able to: a. List the 26 stars in order from closest to farthest, and b. Share your ratio and how you determined it

Designing a Drone

8. Provide time for each group to share what they discovered.
9. Complete the following journal prompt:

    In your opinion, what makes a person have grit?

10. Read chapter eighteen of the novel to students, or ask that it be read independently before the next class period.

Lesson 22

Awesome Idioms

Objectives

- The students will apply the four forces of flight to quadcopters.
- The students will create a personal goal and determine the steps they need to complete it.

Materials

- Chapter eighteen of the book *Dinosaurs, Diggers, and Thieves*
- Timelines
- Cardboard pieces from the previous lesson
- Four straight pins per person

DINOSAURS TO DRONES

- *Awesome Idioms* cards
- Student journals

Assessments

- Journal responses
- Timelines
- Student-created models and presentations

Procedures

1. Review material discussed during the previous class session (e.g., examples of grit from the novel, how to build the first half of the model of a quadcopter, a list of the stars closest to Earth, etc.).
2. Ask students to work with their peers to add major events from the story that took place in chapter eighteen.
3. Ask the students to talk with a partner about how the characters in chapter eighteen demonstrated grit.
4. Write the saying "When it rains, it pours" on the board. Explain that this type of phrase is called an idiom. Ask the students to describe what they think this idiom means (e.g., when one bad thing happens, many bad things happen). Ask the students to describe how this idiom might apply to the story.
5. Give each student one of the *Awesome Idioms* cards attached. Their task is to hypothesize what their idiom means and then research it online. When everyone has finished, ask each student to share.

Awesome Idioms

TEACHER NOTE:

Learning common idioms is very important for English learners. If you teach in a school that has a high population of English learners, consider using frame games or word puzzles that introduce idioms to students in a fun way at the start of each class period.

Here are three resources for you to explore:

- www.puzz.com/stickelsframegames.html
- *Word Bogglers: Visual Words and Idioms* by Dianne Draze
- *Scholastic Dictionary of Idioms* by Marvin Terban

6. Provide 20 minutes for students to work on the choice activities below:

CHOICE A	
Materials:	• Cardboard pieces from the previous lesson • Four straight pins
Directions:	Today, you will finish creating your model quadcopter and use it to demonstrate the four forces of flight. a. Place the four circles on your 6-inch piece of corrugated cardboard in two rows of two. Make sure each circle is touching the circle next to it like in the picture shown below (Figure 22.1): **Figure 22.1** Model quadcopter.

	b. Push a straight pin through the center of each circle in order to secure it in place. Spin one of the circles and keep repositioning them until all spin at the same time.
	c. In order for a quadcopter to hover, all four propellers must be operational. Two of the propellers will turn in one direction and two will turn in the other. Spin one of your circles and see if you can tell which way each circle is spinning.
	d. You should have noticed that the circles that are diagonal from each other move in the same direction. Once all four propellers are moving, a force called *lift* makes the quadcopter rise straight up into the air. Make your quadcopter model demonstrate *lift*.
	e. What goes up must come down. Which of the forces of flight represent this downward force? Make your quadcopter model demonstrate the force of gravity.
	f. We still haven't made your quadcopter model move forward or backward. Determine which of the forces of flight would move the drone forward and which would make it slow down and eventually move backward. Demonstrate both thrust and drag using your quadcopter model.
	g. Using the internet, research how the propellers must turn in order for the drone to spin, roll, or tilt. (Hint: look up the terms *roll*, *pitch*, and *yaw*.)
Assessment:	You must be able to: a. Share how the four forces of flight create the conditions for a drone to fly, and b. Describe and demonstrate the terms *roll*, *pitch*, and *yaw*.

CHOICE B	
Materials:	• Student journal
Directions:	During the previous class session, we discussed the term *grit* as a class. People with grit have a goal they believe in and know the importance of practice and hard work. Watch this video clip or read a short biography your teacher will give you: www.youtube.com/watch?v=2H4zzqbKmtE. Talk about how the individuals demonstrate grit. When you are finished, think about a goal you would like to achieve. Research the steps you would need to take and/or the skills you would need to learn in order to meet your goal. Record this in your journal. If time permits, pretend you are your future self. Write a letter describing what it feels like to successfully achieve this dream.
Assessment:	You must be able to share what your goal is and a few of the steps necessary to achieve it.

7. Provide time for each group to share what they discovered.
8. Complete the following journal prompt:

    When we last met Dorian, he was trapped in the back seat of the thieves' truck. What do you think will happen in the next chapter?

9. Read chapter nineteen of the novel to students, or ask that it be read independently before the next class period.

Name: _____ Date: _____

Awesome Idioms Cards

Awesome Idioms BLIND LEADING THE BLIND	**Awesome Idioms** CALM BEFORE THE STORM	**Awesome Idioms** COOL AS A CUCUMBER
Awesome Idioms DON'T COUNT YOUR CHICKENS BEFORE THEY HATCH	**Awesome Idioms** EAT YOU OUT OF HOUSE AND HOME	**Awesome Idioms** FISH OUT OF WATER
Awesome Idioms GET INTO THE SWING OF THINGS	**Awesome Idioms** HOT UNDER THE COLLAR	**Awesome Idioms** IN THE LIMELIGHT
Awesome Idioms JUMP ON THE BANDWAGON	**Awesome Idioms** KEEP YOUR NOSE TO THE GRINDSTONE	**Awesome Idioms** LOW MAN ON THE TOTEM POLE
Awesome Idioms MIND YOUR P'S AND Q'S	**Awesome Idioms** NUTTY AS A FRUITCAKE	**Awesome Idioms** ON CLOUD NINE
Awesome Idioms PULL THE RUG OUT FROM UNDER YOU	**Awesome Idioms** READ BETWEEN THE LINES	**Awesome Idioms** THROUGH THE GRAPEVINE

Lesson 23

Gyroscopes and Game Plans

Objectives

- The students will explore the importance of gyroscopes to drones.
- The students will begin planning a class competition called *The Grit Games*.

Materials

- Chapter nineteen of the book *Dinosaurs, Diggers, and Thieves*
- Timelines
- Gyroscope toy
- Student journals

DINOSAURS TO DRONES

Assessments

▶ Timelines
▶ Journal responses

Procedures

1. Review material discussed during the previous class session (e.g., examples of idioms, the definitions of *pitch*, *yaw*, and *roll*, etc.).
2. Ask students to work with their peers to add major events from the story that took place in chapter nineteen.
3. Remind students that in this chapter, Zade finds Dorian's drone in his backpack. Ask the students to predict how the diggers might use it to find Dorian and stop the thieves.
4. Explain that almost anything can be used for both good and evil. The diggers are going to use a drone for good, but others have used them to commit crimes. Read the news article linked below or locate a different news article of your choosing: https://www.abc15.com/news/national/drone-hackers.
5. Now, introduce the students to the following idiom: "Don't throw the baby out with the bath water." Ask the students what they think it means and how it applies to the news article and the novel we have been reading.
6. Provide 20 minutes for students to work on the choice activities below:

CHOICE A	
Materials:	• Gyroscope • Student journal
Directions:	In the previous lesson, we talked about how the propellers on a quadcopter must move in order for it to fly. Inside each drone there are two hidden micro-electromechanical systems (MEMS) that control this movement. The first is called a gyroscope, and the second is called an accelerometer. Pick up the toy gyroscope and pull the string as quickly as possible. Watch carefully and observe what happens. Now, rewind the gyroscope and hold it in your hand. Pull the string and then slowly twist your wrist in various directions. What do you notice when you do this? You should feel a small amount of resistance on your wrist. Gyroscopes help to stabilize objects and keep them from falling over. This is called *gyro stabilization*. It's obviously not possible to pack a big object like the gyroscope in front of you inside a drone. Watch the video linked here or read a short article to learn about the type of gyroscope found inside drones: https://youtu.be/zwe6LEYF0j8.

Gyroscopes and Game Plans

Assessment:	You must be able to:
	a. Define *gyro stabilization*, and
	b. Describe the type of gyroscope found inside drones

CHOICE B	
Materials:	• Student journal
Directions:	In just a few short days, the class will be holding a fun competition called *The Grit Games*. During this competition, each person will be asked to solve four challenging tasks within a 30-minute time period without giving up. Your job today is to brainstorm a list of challenges or puzzles that could be included in this competition. Example tasks from previous *Grit Games* are shown below (Figure 23.1): 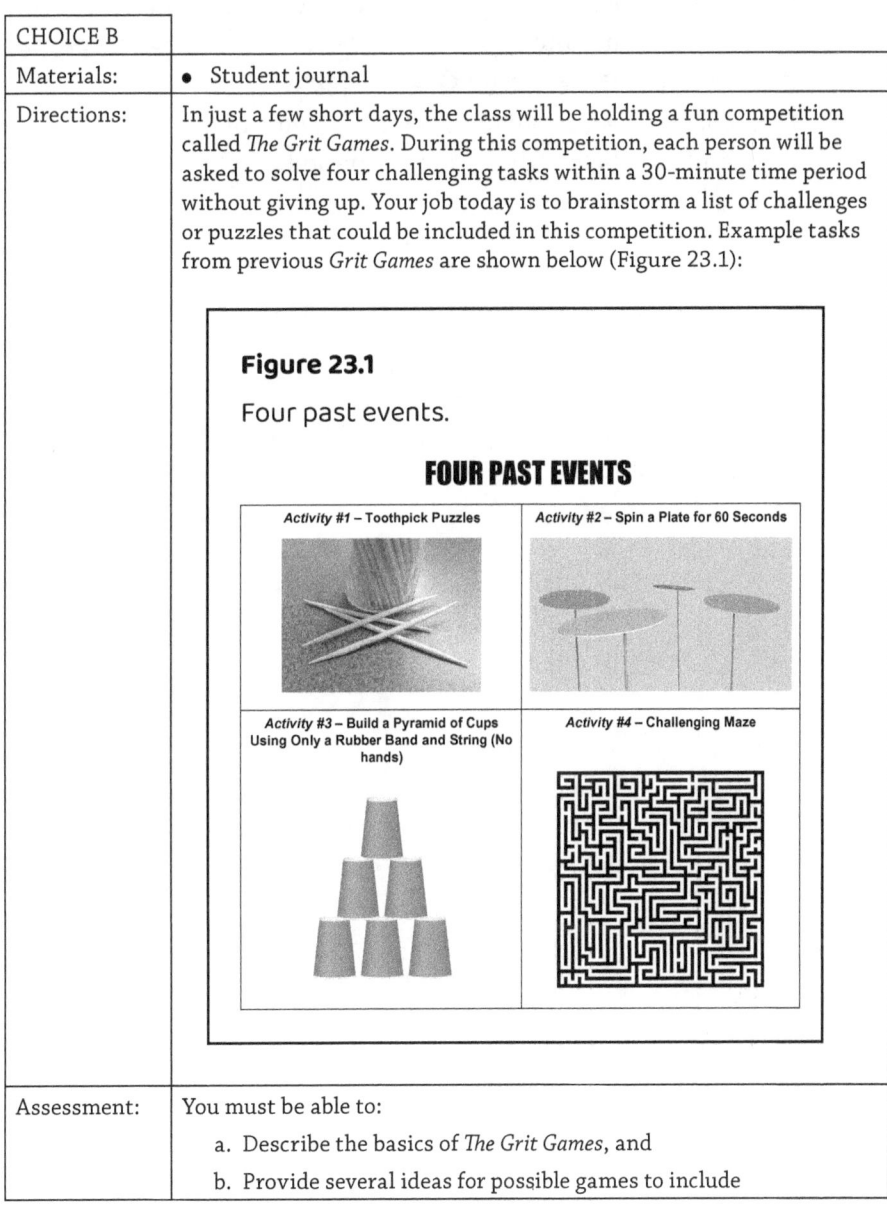 **Figure 23.1** Four past events. **FOUR PAST EVENTS** *Activity #1 – Toothpick Puzzles*; *Activity #2 – Spin a Plate for 60 Seconds*; *Activity #3 – Build a Pyramid of Cups Using Only a Rubber Band and String (No hands)*; *Activity #4 – Challenging Maze*
Assessment:	You must be able to:
	a. Describe the basics of *The Grit Games*, and
	b. Provide several ideas for possible games to include

7. Provide time for each group to share what they discovered.
8. To end the lesson, inform students that during the next class session they will be creating a *breakerspace*. Explain that this is the opposite of a *makerspace*. In essence, students will be able to take various objects apart to see how they work. Request students bring in old unwanted toys or household objects (**with parent permission**) that can be taken apart safely.
9. Read chapter twenty of the novel to students, or ask that it be read independently before the next class period.

Lesson 24

Breakerspace Breakdown

Objectives

- The students will disassemble an object in order to see what is inside.
- The students will make a judgment after listening to multiple perspectives.

Materials

- Chapter twenty of the book *Dinosaurs, Diggers, and Thieves*
- Timelines
- Items to disassemble

DINOSAURS TO DRONES

- *Breakerspace Breakdown* handout
- Screwdrivers of different sizes
- Goggles
- Blank *Official Grit Games Score Card*
- Student journals

Assessments

- Journal responses
- *Breakerspace Breakdown* handout
- Timelines

Procedures

1. Review material discussed during the previous class session (e.g., description of *The Grit Games*, *gyro stabilization*, etc.).
2. Ask students to work with their peers to add major events from the story that took place in chapter twenty.
3. Create four signs that say the following:
    a. Mr. Connor, the Twins, and the Security Guards
    b. Mr. Connor and the Security Guards
    c. The Twins and the Security Guards
    d. The Security Guards Alone
4. Tape one sign in each corner of the room. Instruct students to move to the corner that represents who they believe is responsible for the theft. Each student must make a choice and cannot stand in the middle of the room.
5. Call on one or two students at each sign to justify why they suspect who they chose.
6. After listening to various points of view, give the students an opportunity to change their minds and move to a different corner. If someone changes their mind, ask them to explain why.
7. Read each of the choice activities aloud and allow the students to choose. Explain that anyone who did not bring an object to disassemble must choose option B. Provide 20 minutes for students to work on their chosen task.

Breakerspace Breakdown

CHOICE A	
Materials:	- *Breakerspace Breakdown* handout - Screwdrivers of various sizes - Goggles - Object to disassemble
Directions:	During the previous lesson, we talked about the MEMS inside of a drone. A breakerspace is the opposite of a makerspace. In a makerspace, you build something. In a breakerspace, you take it apart. Closely observe the object you brought to take apart and record your thoughts on part one of the handout your teacher will give you. Once your teacher has verified that your object is safe to disassemble, you may use the screwdrivers and other tools to do so. Make sure to wear eye protection. After it has been deconstructed as much as possible, record what you found on part two of the handout.
Assessment:	You must be able to describe what you discovered inside the object you disassembled.

TEACHER NOTE:

This is an excellent opportunity to truly see change over time from the inside. After students have taken their objects apart, ask them to compare the oldest object that was disassembled with the newest object.

What generalizations can they make? For example, are there fewer electronic parts or more? Are the materials the objects are made of more-or-less durable? This is also a great time to ask your students to complete a row on their *Continuum of Change* chart for their object.

CHOICE B	
Materials:	• Blank *Official Grit Games Score Card*
Directions:	Today you will need to work as a group to finalize the four challenging tasks you think your classmates might enjoy completing during *The Grit Games* competition. Make sure the tasks are not too easy or too hard. When the group has come to a decision, present your ideas to the teacher for final approval. Once your teacher has given his or her approval, examine the sample score card below. Decide what should be included in the four boxes for the approved games. Complete a draft blank score card together. **OFFICIAL 'GRIT GAMES' SCORE CARD** Name _____ Date _____ *Toothpick Puzzles* — How many did you attempt? ____ How many did you solve correctly? ____ *Spinning Plate Challenge* — Record how long you can keep your plate spinning below: Trial #1- ____ Trial #2- ____ Trial #3- ____ *Cup Pyramid* — Record how long your group took to build the cup pyramid using only the rubber band and string below: ____ *Maze* — Have a groupmate verify you completed the maze by yourself without copying by signing their name below: ____
Assessment:	You must be able to share with the teacher your group's draft of a game card.

8. Provide time for each group to share what they discovered.
9. Complete the following journal prompt:

    If you were Dorian, what would you have done in his situation?

10. Read chapter twenty-one of the novel to students, or ask that it be read independently before the next class period.

Name: _____   Date: _____

Breakerspace Breakdown

Description of Object BEFORE Disassembly

Name of Object _____   Brand _____

Intended Purpose of Object:

Sketch of the Object:

Color _____   Size _____

Estimated Cost _____   Estimated Age _____

Is any portion of the object toxic or dangerous?   *(circle one)*   **Yes**   **No**   **Not Sure**

<u>**WARNING!**</u> **If you answered** *yes*, **do not attempt to disassemble the object! If you are** *not sure*, **consult with your teacher.**

If you were to break this object down into each of it's component pieces, how many pieces do you predict there would be? _____

Description of Object AFTER Disassembly

How many parts and pieces did your object consist of?   _____

Sketch the most *interesting* piece in the box below: Sketch the *smallest* piece in the box below:

What surprised you the most about the object you took a part?

What would you still like to know about the object?

Name: _____ Date: _____

OFFICIAL *GRIT GAMES* SCORE CARD	
Game #1	*Game #2*
Game #3	*Game #4*

Lesson 25

Searching for Serendipity

Objectives

- The students will generate examples and non-examples of serendipity.
- The students will calculate the percent of change using a formula.

Materials

- Chapter twenty-one of the book *Dinosaurs, Diggers, and Thieves*
- Timelines
- Calculators
- Student journals

DINOSAURS TO DRONES

Assessments

▸ Journal replies
▸ Timelines

Procedures

1. Review material discussed during the previous class session (e.g., predictions about who committed the theft, breakerspace observations, etc.).
2. Ask students to work with their peers to add major events from the story that took place in chapter twenty-one.
3. Refer back to the sentence in chapter twenty-one that reads: "We should probably check it out though. I'm a firm believer in serendipity." Ask the students to work with a partner and use context clues to determine the meaning of the word *serendipity*.
4. Listen to each group's definition and come to a consensus on a class definition (e.g., events that happen by chance).
5. Next, as a group, generate three examples and three non-examples of serendipity within the novel *Dinosaurs, Diggers, and Thieves*.
6. Provide 20 minutes for students to work on the choice activities below:

CHOICE A	
Materials:	• Calculators • Student journal
Directions:	Mathematicians can calculate the percent of change that occurs in a given situation using a formula. The first step is to subtract the NEW amount from the OLD amount. For example, if a store sold 350 cans of soup last month, but 500 this month, the amount of change would be 500 − 350 = 150. The next step is to insert this number into the numerator (top) of the fraction contained in the formula below: $$\frac{\text{New Value} - \text{Old Value}}{\text{Old Value}} \times 100 = \text{Percent Change}$$ Next, insert the old value into the denominator (bottom) of the fraction. This would look like: $$\frac{150}{350} \times 100 = \text{Percent Change}$$

Searching for Serendipity

	Lastly, you would solve the equation by dividing the denominator into the numerator and then multiplying the decimal that results by 100. The answer would be 42.86%. Use the formula above to calculate in your journal how many gallons of gas are left in the SUV's tank if it began with 12 gallons when it left the ranch but only has 1.5 now. Check your answer with the teacher when you are finished. Finally, create a word problem of your own in your journal and ask a classmate to solve it using the formula.
Assessment:	You must be able to: a. Explain the formula for measuring the percent of change to your classmates, and b. Present them with an original word problem you created to solve

CHOICE B	
Materials:	• Materials for playing *Grit Games* • One piece of blank paper
Directions:	Today you will work as a group to prepare the list of materials the class will need to play *The Grit Games* you have chosen. Place a star next to anything on the list your teacher will need to make copies of and place a checkmark next to anything you need your teacher to purchase or bring in. Prepare in advance anything that can be constructed or compiled today. Next, carefully craft a three- to five-minute presentation you can give to your classmates that explains the rules of each game and what the expectations are for the event. Anticipate ahead of time any questions you think they might have.
Assessment:	You must be able to: a. Share the list of supplies needed with your teacher, and b. Create a presentation outlining the rules for each game

7. Provide time for each group to share what they discovered.
8. Complete the following journal prompt:

    Describe a time when something serendipitous happened to you.

9. Read chapter twenty-two of the novel to students, or ask that it be read independently before the next class period.

TEACHER NOTE:

The novel is now coming close to the end. This is a good opportunity to introduce students to the typical elements of a plot (e.g., exposition, rising action, climax, falling action, and denouement or conclusion). Consider asking students to provide examples from the story of exposition and rising action, and then make predictions about the climax and denouement. Other activities might include creating a plot diagram or thinking through the elements of the plot for a story of their own invention.

Lesson 26

Delineating the Denouement

Objectives

- The students will compare reactions to change from different time periods.
- The students will analyze a chapter to determine which loose ends still need to be wrapped up.

Materials

- Chapter twenty-two of the book *Dinosaurs, Diggers, and Thieves*
- *Continuum of Change* chart
- Timelines
- Student journals

DINOSAURS TO DRONES

Assessments

- Journal responses
- Timelines

Procedures

1. Review material discussed during the previous class session (e.g., the definition of serendipity, how to calculate the percent of change in a given situation, etc.).
2. Ask students to work with their peers to add major events from the story that took place in chapter twenty-two.
3. Provide an opportunity for the students to react to the events in chapter twenty-two through the whip-around technique used earlier in the unit. The sentence frame should be: "*I was most surprised by_____.*"
4. Explain to students that a story typically ends with something called a *denouement*, which is where *all the loose ends are tied up*. Ask the students to list what still needs to be resolved in this book. Make sure to bring up the twins' involvement in the theft if the students do not do so on their own.
5. Provide 20 minutes for students to work on the choice activities below:

CHOICE A	
Materials:	• *Continuum of Change* chart • Student journal

Directions:	Everyone reacts to change differently. For example, here is how Charles and Caroline Ingalls thought about the changes they experienced in the year 1880:
	
	    Ma got up and put another stick of hay on the fire. When she lifted the stove lid, a reddish-yellow smoky light flared up and drove back the dark for a moment. Then the dark came back again. The wild screaming of the storm seemed louder and nearer in the dark.
	    "If only I had some grease I could fix some kind of a light," Ma considered. "We didn't lack for light when I was a girl, before this newfangled kerosene was ever heard of."
	    "That's so," said Pa. "These times are too progressive. Everything has changed too fast. Railroads and telegraph and kerosene and coal stoves – they're good things to have but the trouble is, folks get to depend on 'em."
	    The Long Winter by Laura Ingalls Wilder

Delineating the Denouement

	Your first task is to discuss with a partner and record in your journals whether or not you agree with Pa's statement that "everything changes too fast." When you are finished, research a cutting-edge project in development now. For example, at the time of the writing of this unit, Uber and NASA are working on developing a flying car (http://money.cnn.com/2018/05/08/technology/uber-nasa/index.html). Now, revisit your discussion about whether or not everything changes too fast. Has your opinion changed? Why or why not? How do you feel about the cutting-edge project you researched? Lastly, complete a row on your *Continuum of Change* chart for this project.
Assessment:	You must be able to compare the Ingalls' reaction to kerosene and railroads to your reaction to the cutting-edge project you researched.

CHOICE B	
Materials:	• Student journal
Directions:	*The Grit Games* will take place in a few days. Your task today is to come up with five ways to encourage your classmates if they get frustrated and want to quit during the competition. One example might be to listen for anyone saying, "I can't do this," and add the word *yet* to the end of their sentence for them. Watch a motivational video like the one linked here or read a short article your teacher will give you: https://youtu.be/nalIlgRkABc.
Assessment:	You must be able to share three of your five strategies for developing grit.

6. Provide time for each group to share what they discovered.

7. Complete the following journal prompt:

    If you were Frank, would you have listened to Dorian's advice? Why or why not?

8. Read chapter twenty-three of the novel to students, or ask that it be read independently before the next class period.

Lesson 27

Victoria? Meet Sue!

Objectives

- The students will discover several scenarios involving the legalities of fossil hunting.
- The students will create a product of their choosing to communicate how famous women of the past demonstrated grit.

Materials

- Chapter twenty-three of the book *Dinosaurs, Diggers, and Thieves*
- The book *She Persisted* by Chelsea Clinton
- *Continuum of Change* chart

- Timelines
- Student journals

Assessments

- Journal responses
- Timelines
- Student-created products

Procedures

1. Review material discussed during the previous class session (e.g., the definition of *denouement*, perspectives on the speed of change, etc.).
2. Ask students to work with their peers to add major events from the story that took place in chapter twenty-three.
3. Ask the students to define the word *ironic*. Explain that it means "something happening in the opposite way than expected." Give a few examples (e.g., it only rains a few times a year in Phoenix, but one of those days happened to be when the high school held its graduation ceremony outside, etc.).
4. Instruct students to hold up between one and five fingers (1 = not at all ironic; 5 = extremely ironic) to indicate the level of irony in the situation described in this chapter (i.e., Victoria may be taken away by the government just when they recover her skeleton from the thieves).
5. Tell students that something like this happened in real life. Show students the video clip below or locate an article online about Sue the T-Rex: https://youtu.be/XZywsT8Sy-c.
6. Ask students to determine how the situation the diggers are facing in the novel is similar to Sue the T-Rex.
7. Provide an opportunity for students to debate what they feel should happen with Victoria and why.

Victoria? Meet Sue!

8. Provide 20 minutes for students to work on the choice activities below:

CHOICE A	
Materials:	• Student journal • Computer
Directions:	We have read and discussed how flying drones are being used here on Earth. Now, NASA has developed and used a drone-like helicopter on Mars. Mars has a very thin atmosphere, which is only 1% of Earth's. Think about the four forces of flight discussed earlier. How do you think the four forces of flight play out on a planet with such a thin atmosphere? Record your thoughts in your journal. Next, go to www.nasa.gov and search for the article titled "After Three Years on Mars, NASA's Ingenuity Helicopter Mission Ends." Read this article and describe in your journal a few of the successes and challenges NASA encountered.
Assessment:	You must be able to describe two successes and two failures NASA experienced using a drone-like helicopter on Mars.

CHOICE B	
Materials:	• Student journal • The book *She Persisted* • *Continuum of Change* chart
Directions:	As you know, we have been talking a lot about grit over the last few days. All people face their own unique challenges and must make the choice to persist or give up. Read the book *She Persisted*. When you have finished, choose one of the projects below to complete based on one of the women's lives featured in the book: a. Create a "Grit Superstar Trading Card" b. Write a poem or ballad c. Reenact an event from her life in a skit or pantomime When you are finished, complete a row on your *Continuum of Change* chart for the impact she had on the world.
Assessment:	You must be able to share your product or perform your skit for the class.

9. Provide time for each group to share what they discovered.
10. Complete the following journal prompt:

    What is something ironic that has happened to you that really surprised you?

DINOSAURS TO DRONES

11. Read chapter twenty-four of the novel to students, or ask that it be read independently before the next class period.

TEACHER NOTE:

There have been conflicts over dinosaur bones for decades. Another famous fight over fossils took place in the late 1800s and was dubbed the Bone Wars. Students who enjoy reading about Sue may also enjoy reading about the two paleontologists, Cope and Marsh, who attempted to sabotage each other whenever possible. A fictionalized account of the Bone Wars, as told by their children, is described in the young adult novel *Every Hidden Thing* by Kenneth Oppel.

Lesson 28

Half On / Half Off

Objectives

- The students will debate what would happen if the dinosaur is found to be half on public land and half on private land.
- The students will conduct a poll to determine the percentage of classmates who would have taken advantage of the Homestead Act of 1862.

Materials

- Chapter twenty-four of the book *Dinosaurs, Diggers, and Thieves*
- *Continuum of Change* chart

DINOSAURS TO DRONES

- Timelines
- Student journals

Assessments

- Journal responses
- Timelines
- *Continuum of Change* chart

Procedures

1. Review material discussed during the previous class session (e.g., definition of irony, comparisons between Victoria the Hadrosaur and Sue the T-Rex, etc.).
2. Ask students to work with their peers to add major events from the story that took place in chapter twenty-four.
3. Explain that the characters in the story are facing a difficult dilemma. Hold a debate to discuss what would or should happen if the dinosaur is determined to be half on public land and half on private land. Follow the shared-inquiry steps discussed earlier in this unit.
4. Ask the students to imagine they are a judge hearing the case we just debated. Set a timer for five minutes and ask students to write their verdicts in their journals. Provide an opportunity for a few students to share.
5. Provide 20 minutes for students to work on the choice activities below:

CHOICE A	
Materials:	• Student journal • Computer • *Continuum of Change* chart
Directions:	Use your computer to research the meaning of the word *telemetry*. Record this definition in your journal. When you are finished, find two or three examples of actual studies that were conducted using telemetry. Next, think about what you would choose to study if you could create your own telemetry study. Which part of the world would you focus on, and what species would you track? Lastly, how could someone track change over time using telemetry? Complete a row on your *Continuum of Change* chart for the invention of telemetry.

Half On / Half Off

Assessment:	You must be able to:
	a. Define the word *telemetry* for those who did not choose this activity, and
	b. Explain one example study that used telemetry or describe the study you would like to propose

CHOICE B	
Materials:	• Student journal
Directions:	As you know, Saddle Creek and most of Montana are very rural. Determine the current population of Montana and compare it to California, New York, and your state. Next, read an article like the one below about the Homestead Act of 1862: www.history.com/topics/homestead-act. Do you think you would have been brave enough to move away from your home and take possession of 168 acres of land in the middle of nowhere? Why or why not? Write your answer in your journal. Next, poll your classmates to see what they would have done. Calculate the percentage of those who would have and those who wouldn't have. If time permits, research the name of the legislation that replaced the Homestead Act in 1976.
Assessment:	You must be able to: a. Summarize the key components of the Homestead Act of 1862, and b. Share the results of your poll

6. Provide time for each group to share what they discovered.

7. Complete the following journal prompt:

    Today you had to pretend to be a judge. How do you typically handle making big decisions like this in real life?

8. Read chapter twenty-five of the novel to students, or ask that it be read independently before the next class period.

Lesson 29

The Evolution of Dorian

Objectives

- The students will cite evidence from the text to show how Dorian has changed over time.
- The students will complete the post-test for the unit.

Materials

- Chapter twenty-five of the book *Dinosaurs, Diggers, and Thieves*
- Unit post-test (use the same test included in lesson one)
- The book *Global Warming and the Dinosaurs* by Caroline Arnold
- Timelines

- *Continuum of Change* chart
- Student journal

Assessments

- Journal responses
- *Continuum of Change* chart
- Timelines
- Post-test

Procedures

1. Review material discussed during the previous class session (e.g., the definition of *telemetry*, key components of the Homestead Act, etc.).
2. Ask students to work with their peers to add major events from the story that took place in chapter twenty-five.
3. Remind students that they have had the opportunity to see Dorian grow and change throughout the story. Challenge the class to list as many examples as they can using evidence from the text.
4. Ask the students to complete a row on their *Continuum of Change* chart representing the degree, rate, and quality of change experienced by Dorian.
5. Provide several minutes for students to review their notes and examine their timelines.
6. Distribute and administer the post-test. If anyone finishes early, ask them to complete one of the choice activities below:

CHOICE A	
Materials:	• Student journal • Computer
Directions:	Use your computer to research the term *eminent domain* and write this definition in your journal. When you are finished, discuss the pros and cons of eminent domain with a partner. Next, determine if eminent domain would apply to the situation facing Dorian and his friends. Write why or why not in your journal. Lastly, find two or three examples online of when eminent domain was used for good somewhere in the country.

The Evolution of Dorian

Assessment:	You must be able to:
	a. Define *eminent domain* for those who did not choose this activity, and
	b. List several pros and cons of its use

CHOICE B	
Materials:	• The book *Global Warming and the Dinosaurs* by Caroline Arnold • Student journal
Directions:	One of the major problems the world is facing today is global climate change. Scientists can learn more about the effects of a changing climate by studying the world of the past. Read the book *Global Warming and the Dinosaurs*. When you are finished, answer the following questions in your journal: a. What surprised you about the fact that dinosaur fossils have been found in Alaska and Antarctica? b. How did the dinosaurs deal with a changing climate? c. What can we apply from this book to our own lives?
Assessment:	You must be able to: a. Summarize the book in 25 words or less, and b. Share your answers to the three questions you answered

7. Provide time for anyone who completed a choice activity to share what they discovered.

8. Explain to students that *The Grit Games* they have been preparing for will take place during the next class period.

9. Read chapter twenty-six of the novel to students, or ask that it be read independently before the next class period.

Lesson 30

The Grit Games

Objectives

- The students will participate in *The Grit Games*.

Materials

- Chapter twenty-six of the book *Dinosaurs, Diggers, and Thieves*
- Copies of *The Official Grit Games Score Card*
- Materials needed to play the four chosen games
- A timer
- *Continuum of Change* chart
- Student journals

DINOSAURS TO DRONES

Assessments

- Timelines
- Journal responses
- *Continuum of Change* charts

Procedures

1. Review material discussed during the previous class session (e.g., ways in which Dorian changed from the beginning of the story to the end, the definition of *eminent domain*, etc.).
2. Ask students to work with their peers to add major events from the story that took place in chapter twenty-six.
3. Reference the list of loose ends the class generated in lesson 26 and determine if everything was accounted for.
4. Poll the students to see how satisfied they were with the ending of the book on a scale of 1 to 10 (1 = hated the ending; 10 = loved the ending). Ask for justification from those willing to share.
5. As a class, work together to create three generalizations about the connection between grit and change over time (e.g., change happens no matter what we do, but grit is a choice, etc.).
6. Prepare the room for *The Grit Games* by designating one area of the room for each of the four challenges and setting out the necessary materials.
7. Explain the rules:
    a. The students will have 20 minutes to complete as many of the challenges as they can.
    b. Students can budget their time as they wish (e.g., five minutes for each task or take as long as it takes to complete one, then move on, etc.).
    c. Students can work independently or collaboratively, but cannot give someone else the solution to a task.
8. Start the timer and let students work. At the conclusion of 20 minutes, stop the timer and bring students back together.
9. Go over the solutions with the class.

10. Ask the students to write in their journals about how they demonstrated grit during *The Grit Games*.
11. As a final exit ticket, instruct students to complete a row of their *Continuum of Change* chart while thinking about how they have personally grown and changed from the beginning of the unit until now.

Dinosaurs, Diggers, and Thieves

Figure A.1 Montana landscape.

A novel
by Jason S. McIntosh, Ph.D.

Chapter One

Dorian's back ached, his legs were stiff, and he had a pounding headache. He loved riding the subway back home in Manhattan, but this was another story entirely. What aggravated him the most was that his parents could have easily afforded three one-way airfares from New York City to Billings, Montana and the car rental from Billings to Saddle Creek. The whole 2,000-mile journey could have been distilled down to just eight hours. But, no! They thought it would be more "fun" to take a 30-something hour trip on Amtrak. Under different circumstances, Dorian might have agreed. Deep down he knew his unhappiness had more to do with the destination than the train ride itself. The long journey just gave him more time to imagine how awful his new life was going to be once they arrived.

"They could have at least reserved a sleeping car," he mumbled grumpily to the empty seat beside him. He had given up trying to fall asleep hours ago and instead focused on trying to answer the questions that had played on repeat inside his mind for two weeks now. Who was this recently deceased great-uncle he never knew he had, and why were his parents abandoning everything to take possession of a 1,500-acre ranch in the middle of nowhere? The only ranch his parents had any experience with was the type his mother religiously put on her salads. At least the will had stated they only had to live on the property for one year. On the 366th day, they could sell the ranch and move back to civilization and the life that he loved.

Peering through the crack between the seats, he saw his parents sleeping peacefully in the row behind him. His mother had her head resting on his father's shoulder, her long brown hair covering half her face. Dorian found it unbelievable that they could be so at ease and act as if they didn't have a care in the world.

With a big yawn he turned back around and leaned his head against the window. The coolness of the glass felt good on his sore head. There were so many things he'd rather be doing today: flying his new drone with his best

Dinosaurs, Diggers, and Thieves

friend Steve in Central Park, visiting the Metropolitan Museum of Art... just about anything other than sitting on this train. Would they even have a museum in Saddle Creek? The fact that the population of the entire town totaled just under two thousand made the odds highly unlikely. There were more students enrolled in his former junior high than that!

With nothing else to distract him from his melancholy mood, he let himself sink further into a pit of self-pity and anger. Self-pity because he had been forced to leave behind his best friend, most of his extended family, the advanced tech program he loved at school, and the new apartment they had moved into just seven months before. Anger because he could not understand why his mother was keeping secrets from him. Never in his entire life had she thought it worth mentioning to him that his grandmother had a brother he had never met?

Letting out a heavy sigh, Dorian shifted his attention to the view outside his window. The sun was just peaking over the horizon, shining light onto the patches of blue flax blossoms and yellow goldenrod dotting the hillside. His lack of sleep and general grumpiness kept him from appreciating the beauty of what lay before him. Instead, he shifted his focus to his own reflection looking back at him in the window. His short black hair was sticking up on one side and so he tried in vain to flatten it down. Shifting tactics, he then attempted to make the flat side stand up to match the messy side. This, too, was of no use. He would have to resign himself to looking ridiculous until he could wash his hair or, at least, wet it with a comb. Slipping into the aisle, he decided to make his way to the restroom. The soft pitching of the train from side to side forced him to hold on to the headrests of the seats in front of him as he walked.

Arriving at the bathroom, he discovered it was occupied, as usual. Rolling his eyes, he leaned against the wall impatiently. For whatever reason, the restroom seemed to be the most popular place on the entire train. Maybe it was those little paper cups shaped like ice cream cones next to the faucets that drew people in. The thought of drinking water made his need for the restroom even more urgent. Tapping his foot on the ground, he stared at the door, willing it to open. After three more minutes of waiting, he gave up and decided to try the restroom in the adjoining train car.

Walking toward the large door at the end of the corridor, he pulled it open and stepped into the small tunnel designed to protect passengers as they ventured from one train car into another. Closing it behind him, he quickly realized the cacophony of noise produced by the wheels grinding against the steel of the tracks had been muffled inside the insulated car. Now, only a thin layer of rubber and metal scaffolding separated him from the great outdoors. This did nothing to help his pounding head.

DINOSAURS TO DRONES

Bracing himself, he took three tentative steps forward and opened the door to the adjoining car. Stepping inside, his ears were greeted not with quiet as he had expected, but an equally offensive sound coming from two women in their seventies loudly chatting back and forth. Dorian almost admired the way they effortlessly ignored the nasty looks from drowsy passengers trying to sleep around them. One of the two was obviously hard of hearing because the other kept saying, "Huh? What? Speak up, dear!"

Moving quickly past the talkative seniors, he checked the handle of the second bathroom. Consistent with his recent streak of bad luck, bathroom number two was also occupied. Leaning against the handrail, Dorian crossed his arms in defeat, closed his eyes, and rested his head against the wall. He would just have to wait. To his dismay, he was still in a prime spot to hear all the intimate details of the ladies' conversation.

"Well, as I'm sure you know, my father found those bones decades ago and just never told anyone." The word *bones* caught Dorian's attention and made him open his eyes.

"Sure he did, Roxanne! Just like my brother invented the windshield wiper." The second woman laughed while elbowing the first.

Looking indignant, she replied sharply, "It's true, I tell you!" After taking a few seconds to calm back down she added, "You know I don't like to gossip, but did you hear about Tom and his diggers?"

The second woman smirked at the notion of her friend not being a gossip. "No, but I know you're just dying to tell me."

"Well, Joan, I heard this from Betty down at the general store, and you know she doesn't repeat anything unless it's God's honest truth. He's worried the new owners won't let him dig anymore. They've been working 90 miles an hour to dig her up before they arrive. Oh, those city folk will probably let that place go to wreck and ruin!"

"Don't jump to any conclusions," the second woman warned. "We're a friendly bunch and I'm sure if we go out of our way to be nice to them, they will be nice to us as well." The expression on the first woman's face seemed doubtful. As if to change the subject, she continued on by saying, "Oh, I've been meaning to ask you, how is your sister in St Paul doing?"

"Did you just ask me how my *dinner in the wall is stewing*? That simply makes no sense. Speak up a little, will ya? I just can't hear you anymore. Are you losing your voice?"

Just when Dorian thought he couldn't wait another second, the bathroom door sprang open. He hurried inside, lightly bumping shoulders with the now-aggravated man attempting to exit. Whispering a quick "Sorry!" he closed the door behind him. Perhaps life in small-town Montana was going to be more interesting than he had at first thought. Bones and diggers? Were they really just talking about digging up some woman's bones? Could those two women have been referring to his family and their new ranch? Maybe his great-uncle had been a murderer and that was why his mother had never mentioned him.

Distractedly washing his hands, he left the restroom without remembering to fix his messy hair. Dorian listened carefully as he passed the still-chatting women on the way back to the pass-through to his assigned train car. Unfortunately, they were now discussing the latest cross-stitch technique and barely noticed him as he walked past.

A few moments later, Dorian arrived back at his seat, where he was greeted with an overly chipper "Good morning!" in unison from both his parents. In response, Dorian simply scowled and sat down in his seat with more force than was necessary.

"Got a bee in your bonnet?" his dad asked in an overtly countrified cowboy accent. This was something he had been doing the last three days in the lead-up to Dorian's forced relocation to the Northwest. Not surprisingly, this did little to lighten the mood.

"Oh, Bill. Leave him alone," his mother said, seemingly coming to his defense. "If you don't, I'll just have to *tan your hide*." She said this last sentence with the same pretend cowboy accent her husband had just used.

This time, despite himself, Dorian couldn't help but smile. Seeing her son's reflection in the window, his mother stood up, kissed him on the top of the head, and cuddled back up against her husband. Dorian glanced at his watch and thought, "364 days, 14 hours, and 21 minutes until I'm free from this *hoosegow*." Realizing what he had just thought, he let out an audible groan and covered his head with his hood.

Chapter Two

A loud horn blasted just seconds before brakes began to squeal, signaling their arrival in Saddle Creek. Once the train came to a complete stop, people began to gather their belongings and clog the aisle as they waited to disembark. Dorian remained in his seat, however, using this as an opportunity to catch a glimpse of the town. Unfortunately, a run-down yellow building the size of a small house blocked his view. The paint was peeling off its exterior walls and there was a noticeable dip in the middle of the roof. A faded sign hanging on the large padlocked front door read, "*Train station closed. Use bathroom in general store.*"

His mother's voice interrupted his thoughts. "Okay honey. Let's get moving and please don't forget your iPad."

Dorian was a very responsible person and resented it when his parents treated him like a little child. Most people, in fact, regarded him as mature for his age. Grabbing his duffle bag, iPad secure inside, he stepped into the aisle and followed his parents out the exit and down the stairs. Walking past the edge of the yellow train station, his heart sank as he took in the town that lay before him. It was as if he had traveled back in time. The entire downtown consisted of just one street occupied by no more than a dozen small stores. Not surprisingly, several of the stores looked completely empty. The icing on the cake though was a man on horseback trotting down the middle of the street.

Forgetting that his father had supersonic hearing, Dorian whispered under his breath, "This is it? You've got to be kidding me!"

"Just give it a chance, son," his dad replied. Despite these words, however, Dorian could see apprehension hiding in his father's face as well. Everyone remained quiet until they arrived at the luggage claim and joined the other restless passengers eager to get to their final destination. Glancing down at his watch, his father said, "I hope they hurry. We're supposed to meet a man named Tom in front of the post office at 3:00."

Dinosaurs, Diggers, and Thieves

Winking at his son, he added sarcastically, "Well, at least the post office won't be hard to find."

It took Dorian a second to register the name his father had just used. Hadn't Tom been the name of the man the two older women were talking about earlier this morning? Racking his brain, Dorian tried to remember what else they had said about him. He had some kind of helpers called *diggers* and they were attempting to remove bones from the ground. The anxiety inside his stomach doubled in size.

Dorian's mother, never a fan of sarcasm, replied, "That's enough guys. Keep your chins up. This will be an adventure!" Her eternally positive nature was a great thing, but very annoying sometimes. If a tornado ripped through their apartment, she would inevitably say, "Well, we always wanted a skylight. Didn't we?"

It was 2:43 when the porter opened the compartment and began handing suitcases to waiting passengers. The crowd anxiously pushed forward, but the man with the bags continued to behave as if he had all the time in the world. The whole scene was reminiscent of someone feeding a flock of pigeons in Central Park. Luckily, Dorian's mother had tied a yellow bandana to the handle of each piece belonging to them. This made the process of identification much easier. Altogether they had six suitcases and a large trunk. The rest of their belongings were to be kept in storage back in New York.

Dorian and his father each grabbed one handle of the trunk, his father on the right and Dorian on the left. With their free hands, each pulled a wheeled suitcase behind them. It took two trips, but they managed to carry everything over to the post office right on time. During Dorian's second trip, he had been waiting patiently on the sidewalk for a car to pass by when, for no apparent reason, it stopped to let him cross the street instead. This would have never happened in New York City.

At 3:04 a beat-up gray Ford truck pulled up to the post office. The truck squeaked and rattled into the nearest parking spot and the driver killed the engine. The bed of the truck was almost rusted through and the tailgate was strapped closed with a bungee cord. A tall man wearing a wide-brimmed cowboy hat jumped out and came bounding over with an outstretched hand.

"Howdy, folks! You must be the McAllisters. I'm Tom and here comes my boy Eric." He pointed with his head to the young man behind him. The boy was about Dorian's age and a miniature version of his father, right down to his cowboy hat and boots.

"Glad to meet you," said Dorian's father, gripping Tom's hand firmly. He then returned the introductions. "This is my wife Susan and my son Dorian. Oh, and I'm Bill."

DINOSAURS TO DRONES

Tom shook Susan's hand and moved on to Dorian. He had such a firm handshake that Dorian couldn't help but wince. Eric, on the other hand, simply waved to Dorian and then greeted Bill and Susan with a formal "sir" and "ma'am."

In the best of circumstances Dorian felt awkward around new people. Knowing what he now knew about Tom made his level of discomfort even greater. Perhaps sensing his unease, Tom looked right at him and said, "Well now Dorian, what do you think of our little town so far?"

Clocking the warning look on his mother's face, he paused in an effort to form a sentence that would allow him to neither answer the question honestly nor lie. Luckily, right when he opened his mouth to speak, the train blew its horn once more, signaling its imminent departure. The sudden unexpected blast caused all three newcomers to jump. Susan even made a little gasp and reached for her husband's hand.

Tom chuckled heartily at their reaction and explained, "You'll get used to that soon enough. It comes through every day about this time." Changing the subject, he added, "I guess you all will be mighty hungry. How about some pizza? My treat."

Dorian was indeed starving and felt instant gratitude toward Tom for suggesting an early dinner. The train had relatively good food, but seemed to underestimate the demand for it. Being a vegetarian meant he had to be very selective when ordering. Most of the vegetarian options for lunch had been gone by the time he ventured into the dining car about 11:30.

After loading the luggage into the back of the pickup truck, Tom led the group further down the street. "Will our luggage be okay?" Susan asked Tom as she hurried to catch up with the tall man and his long strides.

"Without a doubt," he answered confidently without looking back.

Many thoughts swirled around Dorian's head as he followed the group. Tom certainly didn't seem like a threat of any kind – quite the opposite actually. About two blocks from the post office Tom abruptly stopped and waited for the others to catch up.

Eric declared proudly, "We're here! This is the world-famous Skinny Joe's Pizza."

Dorian chuckled sarcastically to himself at the thought of anything in Saddle Creek being world famous. The building was a small, two-story structure that looked like it had been someone's home at one point. On the front porch sat two chairs and a small round table still covered with paper plates and used napkins from prior customers. The main entrance to the pizza parlor sat to the left of the lone table. Taking the lead, Eric led the group up the stairs, holding the door open for the three weary travelers and his father.

Dinosaurs, Diggers, and Thieves

The small dining room was empty except for a man sitting by himself at one of the four mismatched tables scattered about. Directly opposite the front door was a counter used for placing orders. Over this hung a lighted rectangular menu board, only half of which actually worked. The lackluster décor did little to take away from the smell of the delicious pizza that filled the air. Dorian's stomach growled loudly, causing Tom to laugh mightily for the second time in less than five minutes.

A very large man wearing an apron smeared with tomato sauce appeared behind the counter and said, "Good afternoon Tom, Eric, and Tom's friends. Everyone calls me Skinny Joe. What can I get for you today?"

Dorian knew there had to be a story here because Joe was anything but skinny. He wasn't overweight either. Instead he could best be described as one large muscle. Dorian's parents smiled at the man and said hello.

"Do you need some time to decide?" Skinny Joe ventured.

"Yes, please," Susan replied. "But first, what are the specialties of the house?"

"Well, my best seller is a thin crust pie loaded from edge to edge with veggies and your choice of elk or bison. We also have a dessert pizza with huckleberries and cream cheese."

Susan politely thanked Skinny Joe and turned to the other members of her family. Before anyone could say anything, Dorian quipped, "I don't care what you say, I'm not eating elk or bison."

Susan simply smiled at her son and asked, "Do you want your usual toppings? Onions, extra cheese, black olives, and pineapple?"

"Sure mom. Thanks."

Tom and Eric ordered the special and decided to go with half elk and half bison. Bill ordered for his wife and son and then everyone headed to a table by the window. Bill and Susan sat facing the window. Dorian took the seat across from his mother and Tom sat across from Bill. Eric pulled a chair over from another table and placed it next to Dorian.

As the adults began to make small talk, Eric looked at Dorian and asked, "So, how was the train ride?"

Dorian could tell Eric definitely had his father's outgoing personality. They were the kind of people who have never met a stranger. Dorian envied that quality in people. He, on the other hand, took a while to warm up and build trust. Maybe that came from living in New York City. It was one of those *"Which came first, the chicken or the egg?"* kinds of things.

"All right," Dorian lied. "I got tired of sitting so much though."

"How long did the trip take?" Eric inquired.

"Thirty-one hours, twenty-seven minutes, and thirty-six seconds – give or take a few seconds. Not that I was counting or anything."

DINOSAURS TO DRONES

Eric laughed and proceeded to ask more about the train ride. Dorian found himself liking this new guy, but wasn't quite ready to let his parents off the hook for dropping a metaphorical nuclear bomb on life as he knew it. There would now forever be life before Saddle Creek and then life after.

"What's New York like? Is it as cool as I imagine?" Eric wondered aloud.

"It's amazing!" Dorian effused. "There is so much to do there: museums, zoos, parks, libraries…you name it. There is a Starbucks on every corner and a theater or art gallery on every other block. We have two football teams, two baseball teams, two basketball teams, and three hockey teams. Every Christmas we have the biggest parade and on New Year's Eve, well, it's the place to be. You wouldn't believe the size of Central Park and the way the skyline looks at night. Once when I was ten…"

Suddenly feeling silly for going on so much, he stopped himself midsentence. Talking about his former home made him feel both sad and comforted at the same time. He liked Eric enough, but he wasn't ready to show all his cards yet.

Seeing a sad expression creep onto his face, Eric said, "Sorry, man. I understand. It must be a huge change coming to a place like this. And then to top it off, losing your uncle so recently! We miss Philip an awful lot. He was a great man. I guess I don't need to tell you that though, do I?"

Dorian didn't quite know how to reply to this last comment. Deciding that the truth was the best option he said, "Well, he was my great-uncle and I never actually met him. You know more about him than I do."

A look of surprise filled Eric's face. It was obvious he wanted to know why, but was too polite to ask. Dorian was thankful because he didn't know why himself. The only answer he had ever been given was, "It's complicated." Feeling as if he was being watched, Dorian glanced over at his parents only to discover his mother staring right back at him. As soon as their eyes met, Susan acted as if she had not been eavesdropping and turned away to study a flier on the wall advertising a rodeo coming to town next month. Dorian noted the oddness of the moment and then turned back to Eric, who had already started talking again.

"Philip was so kind to Dad and me. He loved the outdoors and would do almost anything for you. A few years ago, he single-handedly kept the town from going bankrupt. He wasn't a rich man, but he found a way to do it."

"Well, I'm glad because with all the secrecy in my family lately I thought he might be a terrible jerk or something." Dorian made this last statement fully aware that his mother was probably listening in again. He had a right to say how he felt. If that made his parents uncomfortable, well, so be it. Just then Skinny Joe arrived at the table carrying a tray full of drinks: two

Dinosaurs, Diggers, and Thieves

waters with lemon for Bill and Susan, a Sprite for Dorian, and root beer for Tom and Eric.

"So guys, getting to know each other a bit?" Tom asked the boys.

"Yes sir," answered Eric with a smile. It was then that Dorian realized he knew nothing yet about Eric. His father had always told him that if you don't know what to say to someone ask them something about themselves.

"What do you like to do for fun around here?" Dorian inquired.

"Well, Dad's work keeps us pretty busy, but there's a swim club down the street I participate in a couple times a month. I also like riding horses and four-wheeling, too."

This provided a perfect opportunity to ask what type of work Tom actually did. Before he could speak though, Eric moved on to talking about the other kids in town. Evidently there were 21 kids in his grade at school, 12 girls and 9 boys. He described the high school in very positive terms and said the others were excited to meet him once the new school year began.

By the time Skinny Joe delivered the pizzas, Dorian had relaxed and felt less nervous being around the father and son pair. They seemed like genuinely nice people. He would give them a chance for now and let the intrigue go for a while. Well, at least until tomorrow.

Chapter Three

Dorian had his own personal ranking system for pizza: one star meant it was throw-up worthy, two stars meant it was the same as or better than the school lunch pizza, three stars meant it was awesome, and four stars meant "there were no words." Skinny Joe's pizza was definitely four stars.

After paying the bill and leaving a rather large tip, Tom led the group out of the restaurant and back to the truck. From here they would drive directly to the infamous ranch. This had been a collective decision made over a huckleberry-and-cream-cheese dessert pizza Skinny Joe had recommended the table share.

Dorian had thought nothing could possibly be worse than the neverending train ride he had so recently endured, but he had been sorely mistaken. Sitting on a plywood board in the bed of Tom's rusty old truck eclipsed even the scariest roller coaster he had ever ridden. At first, everything seemed okay as they sped down what qualified as the main road out into the country. About 20 minutes into the journey, things had taken a drastic turn. Paved roads had turned into dirt and gravel paths. The flat terrain morphed into rolling hills and winding pathways he was sure weren't on a map anywhere.

Dorian imagined this must be what it felt like to be on the inside of a pinball machine. Surely, this was illegal: no seat belts, no handles to grip, only wide-open space. Just when he thought his insides were going to come out his nose, the truck began to slow and gradually stop. A gust of wind carried the large plume of dust the tires of the vehicle had kicked up behind them back into the truck. Coughing and sputtering, Dorian attempted to clear his eyes from dust.

Standing up on somewhat wobbly legs, Dorian grumpily demanded, "Where are we?"

Eric simply said, "Your new backyard," and then let the view speak for itself. The truck had stopped at the top of a large hill, affording a

Dinosaurs, Diggers, and Thieves

360-degree panorama. As far as his eyes could see, Dorian saw only craggy slopes and narrow valleys. There was no sign of civilization or human engineering anywhere. Not even trees interrupted the landscape, only small scrub bushes and flowering plants. This was a foreign but amazing sight for someone who had spent his entire life in a city surrounded by people and buildings.

Noticing Dorian's wide-eyed expression, Eric smiled and said, "We're going to make a little detour before heading to the house. Follow me!"

The thrill of the moment quickly dissipated as the conversation he had overhead on the train crept back into his mind. If Tom and Eric were up to something sinister, this would be the perfect place to carry out their plan. Not a living soul could be seen for miles around. Seeing his parents exit the cab of the truck, he made the decision to stay close to them for the time being.

Tom took the lead and wordlessly led the group forward. A short distance from the dirt trail they had been driving on, Dorian could make out what looked like unnaturally disturbed earth. The image became clearer with every step as shapes began to emerge from the rocky soil. Finally, he began to put two and two together and realized he was looking at bones.

For a split second, his worst fears about Tom had come true. Before panic set in, however, he realized something wasn't making sense. The bones were much too large to be human. The largest of the bones were as thick as the top of his arm and stretched about two-and-a-half feet in length. The overall shape of the skeleton was off too. Whatever it was had four legs, a long neck, and part of a tail. Glancing at his parents he saw the same confused looks on their faces.

Rubbing his eyes to make sure he still didn't have dust in them, he stammered, "Is this what I think it is?"

As if on cue, both Tom and Eric said at the same time, "Meet Victoria!"

After the shock wore off, Dorian began to think more clearly. Everything began to make sense: the bones, the diggers, everything! They may not have had a world-class museum in Saddle Creek, but they had something even better – real dinosaurs! Even more astonishing, the dinosaurs were on his family's very own property.

Reveling in their reactions, Tom began to explain what they were looking at. "What you see here is a hadrosaur from the Cretaceous period. Hadrosaurs were herbivores and belong to the duck-billed dinosaur family. They once roamed this area in huge herds. We found Victoria about two years ago now. Wow! I can't believe how quickly time has gone."

Dorian had so many questions, he didn't even know where to begin. Before he could say anything, his father spoke first. "This is amazing! We had no idea. Have you determined how it died?"

Eric corrected Bill politely by saying, "You mean how *she* died. We are pretty sure it was a female. Dad thinks she died near a stream of some kind, but we don't know of what."

Jumping in before someone else could speak, Dorian asked, "Why do you think she died near a stream?"

"It's a safe bet because her skeleton is almost fully articulated," Tom replied.

"Articu-whated?" Dorian asked.

"Articulated. Sorry about that," Tom said, laughing. "You'll learn the lingo soon enough. Articulated means the bones are intact and in the correct position. My theory is that she was caught in a flash flood that partially buried her in the streambed. The only thing left above the ground was the last half of her tail. We found a few pieces of it about 20 feet away. It was over there where you see that stake in the ground," Tom said, pointing. "If she hadn't been covered by sediment and water, she wouldn't have fossilized at all. A scavenger would have eaten her and we would have never known of her existence."

Getting in on the action herself, Susan asked, "Well, what determines if something becomes a fossil or not?"

"It takes four ingredients: water, minerals, pressure, and time," Tom explained.

"And why did you name it Victoria?" Susan continued.

"My late wife was named Victoria. Eric chose the name in his mother's memory."

Dorian glanced at Eric and noticed he had his head done and seemed upset by the mention of his mom's passing.

"I'm so sorry for your loss," Susan said tenderly. "How long has it been?"

"She passed away in May three years ago. It was breast cancer," Tom answered.

"I know so many women who have died of breast cancer. I hope one day soon they will find a cure."

Dorian wished his mother would just change the subject. He hated thinking about death and couldn't imagine losing his own mom. Eric had now turned his back to the group and was kicking loose pebbles with the toe of his shoe.

Bill, obviously feeling the same urge to change the subject, redirected the conversation by asking, "So, how did you end up finding Victoria on Philip's land?"

Tom went on to explain that Philip had given him permission to fossil hunt on his property for two reasons: (a) Tom's extensive training as a paleontologist at the Museum of the Rockies, and (b) the desire they both had to establish a paleontological museum in Saddle Creek. Evidently, the town was in the process of dying economically and in desperate need of tourists to keep it alive.

"Most of the land around here belongs to the government," Tom continued. "Any fossils found on federal land belong to the government too. The only way for me to find and claim a specimen for Saddle Creek is to convince private landowners to allow me to search on their properties."

"Can't you get a permit or something from the government?" Susan asked.

"Yes. I would qualify as a trained professional, but I must agree to display the fossil in an already-approved facility. We haven't built our museum yet because we don't have the money. We won't have the money until we unearth the dinosaur. It's a catch-22."

"I didn't realize how complicated the rules are for collecting on public lands," Bill said.

"Don't get me wrong. For the most part, it's a good thing. Did you know that 12 tons of petrified wood disappear from the Petrified Forest in Arizona every year? Fossil poaching is a big problem."

Dorian's mind again went back to the two women on the train. Hadn't they been concerned about what the "city folk" would do when they arrived?

As if Tom had been reading his mind, he said, "Many people in town were concerned the new owners of the ranch would decide to sell the fossils at auction to the highest bidder or refuse to allow our work to continue altogether. Naturally, as new owners of the ranch, you have the right to do what you think best. I won't try to stop you, but I ask you from the bottom of my heart to think about the town. Think about the people here who desperately need jobs and a reason to wake up in the morning. Think about what Philip would have wanted."

Feeling the emotion in his plea, Bill suggested they talk about it over coffee tonight. With the awkwardness now all out in the open, the group headed back to the truck and onward toward the ranch house.

Chapter Four

Dorian held on tightly as the truck plodded up and down another half-dozen hills on its way toward the ranch house. Initially, Eric had tried to carry on a conversation with him, but the noise of the engine and the tires on the loose gravel had made that practically impossible. Secretly, Dorian was thankful for the time to think. So much had transpired in the last few hours. The conversation to come between Tom and his parents would be interesting for sure. Dorian knew his father was a very reasonable man, but he also knew he was what Susan had dubbed "a studier." He never came to a rash decision about anything. Instead, he preferred to research all options no matter how long it took, unaffected by the inevitable impatience of his wife and child.

A wooden sign about 20 yards ahead brought Dorian back to the present. In less than a minute the truck was close enough for him to read the words "Cretaceous Ranch" fairly clearly. What a funny name for a ranch, he thought. The word sounded familiar, but he couldn't quite remember what it meant. Glancing over at Eric, he noticed he was being watched. The big smile on his face told Dorian that Eric wanted to see his reaction to the sign. He could either smile back and pretend to know what it meant or be honest and display a look of confusion. Choosing to play it cool, he decided to smile back and just research it later.

The ranch house he and his family would live in for the next year was another half mile past the sign. By the time they arrived, the sun had dropped below the horizon making it difficult to make out many of the details. All he could tell at this point was that it was a medium-sized home, most likely gray in color, and a little run down. Dorian hoped it would be better on the inside than the outside. Anxious to get a closer look, he jumped over the tailgate of the truck and headed toward the house.

"Here we are, guys!" Tom proclaimed. "It's not the Taj Mahal, but it will treat you well all the same."

Dinosaurs, Diggers, and Thieves

Bill and Susan looked at each other, swallowed hard, and walked up the short sidewalk to the front door.

"The key is under the mat. Original, I know," Tom laughed.

Bending down, Dorian picked it up and handed it to his father. Once inside, they were greeted by a small family room containing the following: an overstuffed couch, two antique-looking armchairs, a fireplace, and an old-fashioned tabletop television with rabbit ears sitting on a coffee table. The head of an antelope was mounted over the mantle and old family portraits hung over the couch. To the left of the television hung a large map. Stepping closer, Dorian realized it must be a map of the ranch. Knowing what he knew about cartography, he could tell the map had to be at least 50 years old. Making a mental note to study the map later, he joined his parents, who had already moved on to the adjoining kitchen.

"Not bad!" Susan commented. "I'm excited to have a gas stove for the first time. In New York everything is usually electric. My mom always raved about how gas stoves are far superior. We shall see, I guess."

"I'm afraid you'll have to go into town tomorrow to buy groceries," Tom warned. "The only things Philip has left are some dry goods, ground coffee beans, and a couple jars of his famous salsa. I don't know where he picked up his recipe, but it's pretty amazing."

"That brings up a good point," Bill interrupted. "We need to look into getting a truck of our own right away. Any suggestions about who to contact or where to go?"

Seeing this as the perfect time to escape, Eric snagged Dorian and showed him the rest of the house. There was a small dining room, two bedrooms, a mud room, and one bathroom. The house was still full of Philip's belongings, making Dorian feel like he was trespassing into someone else's life. He hoped this feeling would go away. Each room was clean and organized, except for the dining room. Evidently, Philip had used this as his office. Piles of documents covered the table top and two rusty filing cabinets stood in one corner.

"What is all this?" Dorian inquired.

"Your guess is as good as mine," Eric replied. "We didn't have the heart to go through anything yet. He was a kind and generous man, but also a secretive one. He liked his privacy."

"That explains a little of the mystery, I guess," Dorian said. "Do you know of any reason why my parents wouldn't want me to know about him? I mean, you seem to have really liked him. I haven't heard one negative comment yet."

"Honestly, no. He was respected around the community and was a pretty easygoing guy. I think—"

DINOSAURS TO DRONES

"Dorian! Where are you honey?" Susan yelled from the kitchen, interrupting Eric mid-sentence.

"In the dining room, Mom!" Dorian hollered back, disappointed his conversation about Philip had been cut short.

"Can you come here for a second?" she replied.

Both Dorian and Eric joined the adults in the kitchen. Bill addressed the boys in a serious tone, "We want both of you to be in on the conversation we are about to have. Let's all have a seat in the living room."

After everyone made themselves comfortable, Bill continued the conversation. "So, here are the facts as I see them. Philip trusted you two enough to let you conduct a paleontological dig on his property. The town has plans to preserve and display the dinosaur in a proper museum one day, once enough money has been raised. Is there anything else my family needs to know in order to make the right decision?"

Tom looked thoughtful for several seconds and then said, "Not really. I think that sums it up, Bill. I can show you all the documents from the dig site. I can introduce you to the town council and you can question them. Other options you could consider are selling the fossil, donating the fossil to the Museum of the Rockies, or even keeping it yourself. We hope that's not the direction you decide to take, but it's within your rights as the new owners."

Looking over at his wife and son, Bill asked, "What do you think guys? Any questions for them? Speak now or forever hold your peace."

Susan spoke first. "I don't see any reason why we shouldn't keep things the way they are. I know we've just met Tom and Eric, but I for one trust them," she said, smiling over at the eager pair.

"Dorian, what about you?" probed Bill.

An idea struck Dorian like a ton of bricks. No question he was in favor of letting Tom and Eric continue, but he would add one stipulation to the deal. "I agree with Mom, but on one condition." Tom and Eric looked anxious and his parents seemed surprised. "You must agree to take me along with you every now and then to teach me about paleontology."

Tom let out a relieved chuckle. "You got it! It would be my pleasure!"

"Well," Bill said. "As long as you don't hold us liable if anyone gets hurt on the dig site and you agree to Dorian's condition, I think we have an agreement!"

Tom and Bill stood and shook hands at the same time the two boys high-fived.

Chapter Five

Dorian woke up in his great-uncle's former guest room starving the next morning. Hearing voices coming from the kitchen, he stumbled out of bed and pulled on a pair of pants before heading to investigate. Walking around the corner and into the kitchen, Dorian saw his parents, Tom, and Eric munching on bagels and drinking orange juice.

"Well, good morning, sleepy head! I was about to come wake you," his mother trilled.

"What's going on?" Dorian replied.

"Didn't you say you wanted to join Tom and Eric on the dig? They brought breakfast and are ready to go as soon as you get dressed. Your dad and I are going to unpack and work around the house this morning, but you go and have a great time."

So it wasn't a dream after all, Dorian thought. "I didn't know you meant today! Give me five minutes," he said excitedly and then raced toward the bathroom.

The tile floor felt cool under his bare feet as he brushed his teeth and washed his face. It was nice not having to wait in line for the bathroom like the train. Back inside his new bedroom, he changed into his favorite pair of shorts and an old T-shirt, anticipating that he would probably be getting dirty today.

True to his word, he joined the group in the kitchen in just under five minutes. While he was away, his mother had smeared cream cheese on a bagel for him and handed it to him now. Dorian immediately began stuffing his mouth and chewing as quickly as possible. His mother gave him the look all mothers give that means "mind your manners," forcing him to slow down to a reasonable pace.

As Dorian ate, Tom explained they would be joined today by five volunteers from different parts of the country who had paid to work on the dig for a two-week period. He went on to explain that all profits from the volunteer program went directly to the future museum project. As the adults continued to talk about the logistics of the day, Eric began to give Dorian a rundown on the volunteers.

First, there was Jose, a 40-year-old cryptozoologist from New Mexico. According to Eric, a cryptozoologist is "an oddball who believes in Bigfoot, Loch Ness, and junk like that." Dorian could sense the light-hearted sarcasm in Eric's voice and was determined to keep an open mind about Jose.

Next, there was Sylvia. Eric described her as an unbelievable 72-year-old grandmother from Georgia who had volunteered the last three summers. Curious, Dorian asked, "Doesn't she get tired or have trouble climbing up and down all those hills?"

"Are you kidding?" Eric replied. "She gets around better than I do. She has been almost everywhere and done just about everything you could imagine. Believe it or not, I've heard rumors she used to be a trapeze artist for a circus and still practices a couple times a month."

"Cool!" Dorian exclaimed.

Then, there were Alexander and Cassandra, 15-year-old twins from a wealthy family in California. Eric needed only two words to describe them, "Spoiled brats." Although Eric didn't think much of the two, he went on to explain that their father, Mr Connor, had been quite generous. He had agreed to fund an idea Tom had pondered for a long time. It had always been his goal to provide a scholarship to a young person who couldn't afford the $2,000 it took to become an honorary member of the dig.

Dorian could easily imagine the impact a scholarship like that would have on someone. The fact that Victoria was already changing him was proof enough. This brought the conversation around to Zade, the scholarship recipient. He was a 17-year-old honors student from Chicago.

"His mother wrote an email six months ago asking if her son could volunteer this summer," Eric explained. "She said her son was really smart and wanted to be a paleontologist, but she simply couldn't afford the large price tag. I know $2,000 sounds like a lot to charge, but most of the money goes to meals, supplies, and hotel rooms on the outskirts of town. Dad always felt bad about having to turn Zade away, so naturally, he was the first choice."

"Well, men," Tom interrupted. "We're burning daylight! It's time to hit the road."

Dorian said a quick goodbye to his parents and eagerly followed Tom and Eric to the truck. Despite the sunshine, he was surprised at how cold it was this morning. Excusing himself, he ran back inside to grab his jacket. This had given him an opportunity to get a better look at the outside of the house. It had two gables, a wraparound porch, and an unusually large chimney. Overall, he thought it was old-fashioned, but quite nice.

Dinosaurs, Diggers, and Thieves

After retrieving his jacket, he squeezed into the cab of the truck next to his new friend. "It will get hot soon enough," Eric warned. "And, there are no trees to find shade under either, so enjoy this while you can."

About five minutes into the trip, Tom slowed to a crawl and pointed out a group of flat stones arranged in a large circle. Evidently, this was an ancient teepee ring made by Native Americans who once called this place home. Dorian's imagination went wild thinking about what life must have been like back then. Twice during the remainder of the trip the truck startled an antelope, sending it pronking over the nearest hill.

Feeling more at ease around the pair, Dorian decided to ask his question from yesterday. "Why did Philip call this place Cretaceous Ranch?"

"Well, Philip came to love dinosaurs almost as much as we do," Tom explained. "He decided to change the name of his ranch to the time period when the dinosaur species we find on his land roamed the earth."

Once they finally arrived at the dig site, Dorian saw a red van parked nearby. "Will you look at that!" Tom exclaimed. "They beat us here today. Oh, Dorian, this was another way Philip helped us out. He lent me the money to pay for the van a few summers ago. I was just about to pay off the loan, when…" His voice broke off, but Dorian could fill in the blanks.

Exiting the truck, Tom jogged over to the waiting passengers still sitting inside the van.

"This is day five for them," Eric explained as the boys exited the truck. Seeing anxiety creep into Dorian's face, he quickly added, "No worries. Just follow my lead. You'll catch up and be an old pro in no time!"

Joining Tom, the boys approached the rear of the van and began to help unload tools and supplies. Dorian's first glimpse of the twins pushing and shoving one another in an attempt to be first out of the van explained why Eric had called them brats. Dorian deduced the next person out of the van had to be Sylvia. She looked as eager as a kid in a candy store and almost as young. Her face had just the tiniest hint of wrinkles and her long white hair was gathered into a ponytail. Noticing the boys at the back of the van, she greeted them warmly saying, "Morning, friends! Ready to get this show on the road?"

The slogan on the T-shirt worn by the next individual indicated it was Jose, the cryptozoologist. "Champ: The Loch Ness of Lake Champlain" was emblazoned across his chest. Stretching and yawning loudly, he joked with Sylvia, who was already ten feet in front of him, "Slow down, coneja! We all aren't as spry as you, you know."

Sylvia turned around good-naturedly and replied, "Ándale, Jose! Ándale!" clapping her hands in rapid succession. Dorian knew instantly he would like both of them a lot.

DINOSAURS TO DRONES

By process of elimination, the last one out of the van could only be Zade. He was African American, about a foot taller than Dorian, and very strong.

"Morning Zade," hollered Tom before he could get too far. "I could use your help carrying the cooler, if you don't mind."

"Absolutely," he replied, joining Tom and the two boys at the rear of the van. Dorian noticed he lifted the cooler packed with ice and other provisions as if it were a paperweight. Very impressive, he thought to himself.

Seeing Zade and Jose had helped Dorian put a finger on something that had been bothering him since his arrival in Saddle Creek the previous day. He hadn't recalled seeing anyone in town who wasn't Caucasian. New York City was such a diverse place that being around all this sameness had made him feel as if something was missing. Now, he would feel a little more at home.

His thoughts were interrupted when Tom greeted the group. "Good morning and welcome to day five. This is Dorian and he will be joining us for the rest of the summer. His parents are the new owners of Cretaceous Ranch and have been good enough to let us continue to dig on their property. They even brought us some extra help," he said, pointing at Dorian. "How's that for good luck?"

Everyone smiled and cheered at this announcement except for the twins.

"Now, let's divide into two groups," Tom continued. "One group will help me with Victoria and the other will go scouting for new finds over on the western side of the ranch."

Alexander was the first to speak. "I'm staying here! It's not like we're going to find anything new anyway. The only bones I've found on this stupid trip have been junk. If I had known that, I would have saved myself the trouble and bought some cool fossils off eBay."

Ignoring the negative tone of his comment, Tom replied, "Well, you never know what you're going to find. Paleontologists discover on average six new species of dinosaur every year. In fact, many of the people who have gotten lucky have been kids about your age. In 1993, a 15-year-old named Sherry Flamand found the most complete Maiasaura ever found. That same year, a 14-year-old found the first dinosaur egg ever discovered in western Colorado. But, it's your call, Alexander."

In response, Alexander grumbled under his breath, kicked the dirt, and crossed his arms. His red hair and freckled skin made him look even more temperamental than he probably was.

Eric whispered, "He's only happy when he's spending money or rubbing in the fact that he's got money to spend."

Dinosaurs, Diggers, and Thieves

Tom then looked over at Eric and said, "Oh! Speaking of kids finding dinosaur bones, Eric wants to show you all one of his prized possessions before we disperse for the day."

On cue, Eric reached down toward his backpack, fished inside and pulled out a large tooth wrapped tightly in cloth. "This is the tyrannosaurus tooth I found last summer after all the volunteers went home."

The tooth was about six inches long and had pointed ridges running its length. Everyone commented on how cool it was, even the twins.

This prompted Dorian to ask, "Does this mean you will one day find the rest of the T-Rex this came from?"

"I wish," Eric said. "But chances are…no. Tyrannosaurs lost their teeth like sharks. When one fell out, they just popped a new one in its place. Most likely this tooth fell out while it was eating. Oh, and we don't know if it was a T-Rex. There are several species of tyrannosaurs."

Dorian suddenly realized how little he actually knew about dinosaurs. Up until this point, his formal education on the subject had consisted of a month-long unit in third grade, a couple documentaries on television, and several visits to the natural history museum. Today was going to be amazing and he couldn't wait to get started!

Chapter Six

After everyone had closely examined Eric's tooth, the team divided into two groups as requested. Alexander, Zade, and Jose chose to help Tom with Victoria. Eric, Dorian, Cassandra, and Sylvia elected to go scouting.

Leading his group down the hill, Eric said, "You know what we want to find today, don't you?"

On cue, Sylvia and Cassandra started chanting, "Theropod! Theropod! Theropod!"

Not knowing what this meant, Dorian asked, "What's a theropod?"

Sylvia patiently explained, "It's a carnivorous dinosaur. Fossil remains of theropods are unbelievably rare. In fact, scientists estimate there were ten to 20 plant eaters for every one meat eater. Theropods are my favorite, too, because they were so cunning and vicious."

Dorian couldn't imagine his grandmother ever liking how *vicious* carnivorous dinosaurs were. When she was alive, she practically fainted at the mere hint of a disagreement between family members. Visualizing the life and death struggle between two multi-ton extinct giants would have pushed her right over the edge.

"The first thing you need to know, Dorian, is where to look for dinosaur bones out here," Eric said pointing to the vast open country in front of them. "The most likely place to find fossils from the Cretaceous age will be on the sides of these hills and cliffs. Since it's too difficult to climb around up there for long periods of time, you'll want to look for bits of bone that have eroded out of the hills and rolled down to the bottom. That's where we start our search; at the bottom of the coulees."

"The bottom of what?" Dorian inquired.

"The coulees," Sylvia repeated for Dorian. "*Coulee* is based on a French word that means 'to flow' and describes the way this land has been carved and shaped into ravines and channels by water over thousands of years."

Dinosaurs, Diggers, and Thieves

"Once you find a small piece of bone at the bottom," Eric continued, "you trace it to its source higher up on the hillside. It's called *following the bone trail*."

"It kind of reminds me of working a crime scene," Sylvia added. "Just like when I was an investigator for the FBI."

This statement took Dorian a minute to process. "You worked for the FBI?"

"It was a brief stint, but yes," she explained. "I can't say much more than that. Top secret you know."

Evidently Sylvia really had done a lot in her life, Dorian thought.

Finally reaching the bottom of the coulee Victoria was perched on, Eric paused the group and described how all objects are naturally pulled down toward the center of the earth due to gravity. Therefore, when a piece of bone reaches the surface and breaks off, it rolls down the hill in a predictable pattern, usually diagonally.

Out of the corner of his eye, Dorian noticed Cassandra glaring at the group with her arms crossed over her chest. "Didn't we already go over this four days ago?" she accused. "It's not fair that you are taking up my time because someone was late to the group!"

Eric gritted his teeth and took a deep breath before replying. "Why don't you go over there, Cassandra, and start searching while we finish up here. Do you think you can manage that by yourself? Or, is that too complicated?"

With a huff, she stormed off in the direction Eric had pointed, muttering something under her breath.

"Wow," Dorian said. "She's quite grumpy this morning."

"Get used to it!" Eric replied.

Redirecting the conversation back to fossil hunting, Sylvia said, "Anyway, all you have to do is find a bit of bone or fossil at the base of a coulee and then follow it up until you, hopefully, find its source."

"Nothing to it!" Eric quipped.

They made it sound so easy, Dorian thought. The next logical question came to him, "But, how do I know if something is a fossil or just a rock? There are tons of rocks and pebbles everywhere I look. You can't possibly check every one."

"Good question," Eric commented. "You want to take this one Sylvia?"

"Sure. Okay Dorian, go ahead and turn around for a minute."

Feeling a little silly, Dorian turned his back on the pair, looking in the direction they had just come. About a minute later, Sylvia said, "You can turn around now. Somewhere on the ground in front of you is a fossilized bone fragment. Can you find it?"

DINOSAURS TO DRONES

Scanning the ground, his first thought was how similar everything looked. Some of the stones were round and some were jagged. Some were large and some were small. The rocks ranged in color from white to gray and every color of brown imaginable. After several minutes of intense study, he was forced to surrender, saying, "I just don't see anything out of the ordinary. Are you sure there's a piece of bone here?"

"Yes sir!" Sylvia chirped. "I placed it there myself. It's about the size of a quarter."

Reaching done, Eric picked it up and held it out to Dorian to hold. "Look at it closely. Do you see how the grooves make a pattern?"

"Yeah, I do. It almost looks like a sponge or coral or something," Dorian said.

"You got it! When you see that pattern, you know you have found something that warrants a closer look," Sylvia added.

"Watch out for concretions though," Eric warned. "They aren't fossils, but are round and can be deceiving."

"Okay. Show me the next time you see one so I'll know," Dorian asked.

"No problem," Eric replied. "Oh, if you are still not sure if something is a bone or not, you can do this." Eric then took the piece of fossil from Dorian's hand and stuck it right on the tip of his tongue. It stuck there as if it had been glued.

Dorian was surprised at what he had just witnessed and burst out laughing, saying, "What in the world are you doing?"

Removing the fossil so he could speak again, Eric explained. "A rock won't do that. Bones have small holes or pores in them that act like mini suction cups."

"Cool!" Dorian replied. "I never thought I'd be tasting rocks today."

"You're disgusting, Eric!" Cassandra scolded. Apparently, she had gotten bored and decided to join the group again without anyone noticing. "That's so gross. You have no idea where that's been!"

The two boys simply looked at each other, rolled their eyes, and began walking with Sylvia in the opposite direction.

"One more piece of advice." Eric offered. "If you want to find large pieces of fossils, walk at a steady pace while scanning the ground. If you want to find small teeth, like from a triceratops, then walk much slower or sit in one place and sift through the dirt."

"Gotcha," Dorian said. "Thanks."

About 15 minutes later, the four hikers arrived at the designated scouting location. Eric divided the area into four sections. Cassandra took section one, Sylvia took section two, Eric took section three, and Dorian took section four. Agreeing to meet back together in one hour, each person headed off on their own.

Dinosaurs, Diggers, and Thieves

Dorian couldn't wait to try out the new techniques he had just learned. Who knew? Maybe he would be the next person in the history books to discover a new species. Anything was possible, but one thing was for sure. To him, Montana and Cretaceous Ranch were awesome. He still missed New York City and his friends, but for the first time in a while now, Dorian felt truly happy.

Chapter Seven

"Ahhhhhhh!" came a bloodcurdling scream from somewhere west of where Dorian had been searching for fossils. Running toward the sound, Dorian spotted Eric rapidly climbing down from his perch on the side of a coulee.

Deciding to wait for him, Dorian hollered up to Eric, saying, "What's going on?"

"That sounds like Cassandra," Eric answered. "She could be in trouble. Let's go!" Without another word, both boys ran in the direction the scream had originated from. It would be hard to know for sure if they were headed to the right spot because of the way sound echoed off the cliff walls. Rounding the next bend in the trail, they caught a glimpse of Sylvia in the distance making her way toward the scream as well.

"HELP!" Cassandra screamed a second time.

Running even faster now, the boys covered half a mile before finally seeing her. She was standing perfectly still with her eyes wide, staring at something on the ground. Inching forward, Eric whispered, "What is it? Is it a rattlesnake?"

After a brief pause, Cassandra squealed, "No! It's worse! It's one of those horned toads and it jumped at me!"

If looks could kill, Cassandra would have died right then and there. "You have got to be kidding me!" Eric yelled. "You screamed bloody murder over a harmless toad?" Stomping forward, Eric bent down and grabbed the toad before it could hop away.

Just then, Sylvia came around the corner, quite out of breath. "Is everything…okay…over…here?" she panted, not looking as spry as she had a few moments ago.

"No!" Cassandra hollered. "That horrible toad was chasing me!"

"Good Lord, child!" Sylvia quipped. "You about gave me a heart attack. I thought you fell or stepped on a rattler. You just can't do that to an old broad like me."

Dinosaurs, Diggers, and Thieves

Simply out of spite, Eric walked toward Cassandra holding the toad in front of him, saying innocently, "Don't you want to see your new friend up close?"

Naturally, Cassandra screamed again and ran further down the path before stopping. The remaining trio burst out laughing despite themselves. Dorian took the opportunity to get a closer look at the toad and then Eric set it free.

Seeing this, Cassandra yelled, "Did you seriously just let it go? What if it comes back? Your dad will hear about this when we get back, Eric. Mark my words!"

Instead of wasting his energy on a response, Eric just shook his head, glanced down at his watch, and announced, "It's time for lunch anyway. Let's head back."

The three turned around and headed back the way they had come. Cassandra hollered from her spot about 50 feet away, "You better not leave me! Where are you going?"

Eric pretended not to hear her and kept walking. Right before they rounded the corner, they heard one last comment from Cassandra. "Jerks!" she yelled.

As they continued their hike back, Dorian noticed out of the corner of his eye that Sylvia was walking with a mild limp. "Are you okay?" he asked.

"Oh, I'll be fine. Just twisted my ankle a bit rushing to Cassandra's aid. Unfortunately, I think I'm going to have to avoid climbing any coulees for a couple days. I can walk, obviously, but I don't want to press my luck and risk putting myself out of commission for the rest of the trip. I'll just stay with Tom and work on Victoria this afternoon and probably tomorrow as well."

"But you love scouting for new specimens," Eric countered.

"I know, but it is what it is," she said. Dorian could sense the disappointment in her voice.

Cassandra interrupted the conversation when she rejoined the group and announced, "Just so you know, I'm not speaking to any of you the rest of the day!"

This news did not have the intended consequences. The boys were thrilled at the prospect of enjoying a Cassandra-free afternoon and the big smiles on their faces showed it. She pouted and complained under her breath for the next ten minutes.

"I see now what you meant about it getting hot out here!" Dorian said.

"Right? It's kind of deceiving in the mornings. What do you think of everything so far?" Eric asked.

Not missing a beat, Dorian chirped, "It's awesome! I love this."

DINOSAURS TO DRONES

"Cool. Glad to hear that. It's not for everyone, but it sure beats a summer job or laying around on the couch watching TV," Eric replied.

Thinking about lounging on the couch led Dorian to think about how he usually spent his free time in New York City. He'd probably be in Central Park today with Steve, messing around with the drone he had saved for 15 months to buy. It had cost him $149. It wasn't his first choice, but it was decent and had a camera built in. Plus, it was small enough that it could be packed into the trunk they had brought with them on the train.

Thinking about his drone gave him an idea. "Sylvia, what if I bring my drone tomorrow? You can walk with us until your ankle bothers you and then use the camera on the drone as a second pair of eyes. If you find something that needs investigating, you can call one of us over and we can do the climbing."

"Great idea!" Eric said.

Sylvia took a few moments to think about this proposal and then responded saying, "Why not? I've always wanted to play around with one of those things. I got my pilot's license when I was 64, you know. I've heard drones are going to take over the skies one day. Not sure how I feel about that."

Rounding a corner, the group was relieved to see the old Ford truck and red van in the distance. Five minutes later they were munching on sandwiches while catching up with the other half of the group.

Chapter Eight

"How'd it go out there, gang?" Tom asked Dorian, Eric, Sylvia, and Cassandra.

"Didn't find much," Sylvia answered. "Just a few scraps. I followed one promising bone trail, but wasn't able to find the source."

"Oh, Cassandra found something, all right!" Eric teased. "Why don't you ask her about it Dad?"

"Shut up Eric!" Cassandra growled.

A glance at Alexander's expression told Dorian he couldn't wait to hear the details. He seemed eager to have new dirt on his sister.

After finishing lunch, it was decided that Eric's group, minus Sylvia, would head east this time. "Don't forget your sunscreen and bug spray," Tom reminded them. "And drink lots of water!"

"We will, Dad. See you soon!" Eric answered and then led Dorian and Cassandra down the hill in the agreed upon direction.

"Good luck!" Sylvia said, waving goodbye with one hand and massaging her ankle with the other.

Dorian couldn't help but feel badly that Sylvia had to stay behind. Glancing at Cassandra to see her reaction, he realized she didn't care in the least that her actions had put Sylvia out of commission. "Did Cassandra even apologize?" he whispered to Eric.

"If she did, I didn't hear it," Eric replied.

Not knowing what else to say, the boys simply shook their heads at her rudeness and continued onwards. They didn't have an opportunity to talk much about it anyway because Cassandra seemed to be staying unusually close to them. Evidently, her experience this morning with the toad had caused her to tiptoe around as if something was going to jump out and bite her any second. Taking advantage of this, Eric found humor in periodically kicking a rock or stick into the brush that lined the path. The rustling noise this created inevitably sent Cassandra bouncing away in fear for her life.

DINOSAURS TO DRONES

In one of the moments when they were alone, Dorian asked Eric, "So, have you ever found anything really big?"

"Well, I found the radius of a hadrosaur about a month ago. It was in three pieces and I had to glue them together then seal them with Vinac. Vinac, or PVA, is short for polyvinyl acetate and is used to harden and protect fossils. It also keeps them from turning yellow with age. The old-timers used to use this stuff that looked really bad over time."

"I would be happy just finding a piece like you hid on the ground for me this morning," Dorian said.

"Ah, that stuff we call *chuck-a-saurus*."

"What?" Dorian replied laughing.

"Chuck-a-saurus," Eric repeated. "It's not worth keeping, so we just *chuck* it through the air. Not when you can find whole skeletons like Dad does."

In moments like these, Dorian couldn't help but notice the admiration Eric held for his father. Soon enough, all talking came to an end as their search began in earnest. Dorian, full of hope and optimism, had one goal for the afternoon. More than anything he wanted to find something cool to show his parents that evening. Concentrating diligently on the ground in front of him, he slowly walked along the base of a coulee.

After just five minutes of searching, beads of sweat began to form on his forehead. A single droplet rolled down his nose and fell to the dirt below. The appearance of a small wet spot drew his eyes toward its location and then what lay nearby. It was an object about the size of a Lego, covered with a wavy pattern similar to the bone Eric and Sylvia had used as a teaching tool earlier that day. His heart began to race as he bent down to pick it up. Thinking back, he knew exactly what he had to do. Checking to see if anyone was looking, he dusted it off and carefully placed it on his tongue.

An outsider would have thought Dorian had lost his mind when he suddenly began running toward Eric while speaking unintelligibly. "Ook! It icks! It icks!" Seeing Eric's confused expression, he removed the bone and screamed, "It sticks! I found a piece of bone! It sticks to my tongue just like you said it should."

Before responding, Eric came closer and examined what Dorian had found. Turning it over in his hand he finally answered, saying, "Good job, Dorian! You definitely found a bone!"

Not able to control his excitement, Dorian leapt for joy and babbled on without taking a breath. "Really? Awesome! I can't wait to show my parents. This is so cool! Steve will never believe this."

As soon as Eric could get a word in again he continued, "Yes, you found a bone. The bone of a rabbit that died, oh…probably six months ago."

Dinosaurs, Diggers, and Thieves

Dorian's grin faded instantly and he began to spit on the ground. Eric laughed amiably, put his arm around Dorian, and said, "Better luck next time, buddy! Better luck next time."

When Tom and Eric dropped Dorian off at home that evening, he was surprised at how exhausted he was. His plans to explore the house a little more would have to wait until tomorrow. Stepping inside, it was obvious his parents had been busy in his absence. Upon entering the kitchen he saw his mother washing shelves and cabinet doors with a soapy rag.

"Dorian!" she exclaimed. "How are you, honey? Did you have a good time?"

"You bet! It was amazing!" he answered.

"That's wonderful, sweetheart!" she replied. "I want to hear all about it. But, not until your father joins us." Carefully stepping down from the stool she was standing on, she walked into the main hallway and hollered down to the master bedroom. "Bill? Come here. Dorian's home and he wants to tell us about his day."

A few seconds later, Bill entered the kitchen, gave his wife a peck on the check, and said, "Let her rip, partner!"

This time, hearing his father's pitiful attempt at sounding like a cowboy didn't annoy him quite as much, and he jumped into summarizing his day. Bill and Susan caught each other's eyes several times during Dorian's ten-minute monologue, surprised at their son's new, improved attitude.

After having their questions sufficiently answered, Susan stated, "You must be starving! All we have for dinner tonight is leftover pizza from Skinny Joe's. I hope that's okay."

"Perfect!" he replied. "I love Skinny's Pizza."

His mom moved to turn on the old gas oven to let it preheat, but Dorian couldn't wait. He grabbed the pizza out of the refrigerator and began eating it cold.

Shaking her head and smiling at her son, Susan said, "Tomorrow, an old ranch hand of Philip's is going to take us into town to look for a jeep or something. We'll go to the grocery store then."

"Any preference, son?" Bill asked. "Jeep or truck?"

He was too busy eating to respond and just shook his head no. In the middle of his third slice, he found he could hardly keep his eyes open. It was barely 8:30, but he was ready for bed. Tom and Eric were going to pick him up tomorrow morning at 7:15 and he wanted to be full of energy. He was especially excited because Tom had asked him to help with Victoria instead of scouting with the others and he couldn't wait. His final thought as he drifted off to sleep was a wish that the rest of the summer would be as brilliant as today had been.

Chapter Nine

BEEP! BEEP! BEEP! Dorian's alarm on his iPhone went off at 6:45 a.m. This time he was going to be ready before Tom and Eric arrived. He slid out of bed, took a shower in the old claw-foot tub, and brushed his teeth. While getting ready he could hear his mother in the kitchen making what was left of Philip's coffee.

Walking into the kitchen, he greeted her warmly. "Good morning, Mom!"

She jumped about a foot off the hardwood floor and then giggled at her own reaction. "You startled me! Aren't you the early bird today?"

"I'm hungry. Do we have anything for breakfast?"

"Well, just the cereal bars we brought with us on the train," she explained. "Tonight, though, I'm going to cook a huge dinner with all our favorite foods."

"Great!" Dorian replied. "That means mac and cheese, right?"

"You got it! Any other special requests?" She soon regretted asking him this question on an empty stomach. Once her grocery list reached three pages she cut him off.

Dorian ate his cereal bar while chatting with his mother, but kept one eye on the cast iron clock over the sink. When the time read 7:30 and they hadn't arrived, Dorian asked her, "Do you think they forgot about me?"

"No dear. I'm sure they haven't. Just be patient," she reassured. But, when another hour had passed and there was still no sign of them, she doubted her own words.

Bill joined his family in the kitchen about 8:35 and offered a potential solution. "Unfortunately, there's no way for me to contact them because cell phones don't work out here. Chris, the ranch hand, will be here soon, though, and I'm sure he won't mind driving you by the dig site on our way to go vehicle shopping in town."

Dinosaurs, Diggers, and Thieves

The minutes continued to crawl by with no word from Tom and Eric. Dorian was getting more and more anxious with each passing second. At 8:57 the sound of a vehicle was heard approaching the house. Running outside, he was disappointed to find it was an old 1970s red Chavelle and not Tom's Ford truck.

Bill joined Dorian outside and waited for a gray-haired man to exit the vehicle once it came to a stop. "You must be Chris," Bill said, warmly greeting the newcomer.

"Why, yes I am. Nice to meet ya," the man replied and then shook Bill's hand.

Dorian, however, deciding now was not the time for pleasantries, elbowed his dad and awkwardly mouthed the words, "Ask him about the dig site."

"Excuse my son," Bill apologized. "He's a little excited to join Tom and Eric today. Do you mind driving by the dig site?"

"I don't mind at all. Jump inside!" Chris replied good-naturedly.

Due to the size of the ranch, it would take almost ten minutes to get there. Bill and Chris made small talk as they drove, but Dorian sat quietly, keeping his eyes peeled for his new friends. Once he did spot the blue Ford truck and the red van, he was surprised to see they were joined by a third vehicle – a sheriff's car. This was not what any of them were expecting.

"I wonder what's going on?" Bill asked.

"I don't know, but we are about to find out," Chris answered.

As soon as the Chavelle finished struggling up the hill and Chris put it in park, all three jumped out and walked toward the scene that lay before them. The volunteers were still sitting inside the van, but Tom was engaged in a serious discussion with the sheriff near his truck. Getting closer, Dorian could hear the conversation as it unfolded.

"I just don't know what I can do, Tom," the sheriff said. "We will keep a lookout for anything strange and I'll contact the neighboring towns, but this is a huge county. We can't leave someone here just to guard your dinosaur. We are understaffed as it is. I'll ask around and spread the news and, hopefully, someone will have seen something."

Dorian could tell the sheriff was being sincere.

"I understand that, but this is Saddle Creek," Bill countered. "Things like this don't happen here. You must have some suspects! Any suspicious out-of-towners hanging around lately? Someone making trouble in town? Anything at all?"

Once again, the sheriff looked disappointed at what he had to say. "No, I'm sorry. And, I hate to say it, but there's not much evidence to collect here either. Just some tire tracks and a couple footprints."

DINOSAURS TO DRONES

Out of the corner of his eye, Tom finally noticed Bill, Dorian, and Chris standing a short distance away. Looking utterly defeated, he excused himself from the sheriff and approached them.

"What's going on?" Bill asked before he could explain.

"Last night someone came onto your property and stole Victoria's skull, as well as a large portion of her front legs. You didn't happen to see or hear anything unusual last night, did you?"

"That's awful Tom," Bill replied. "I didn't hear a thing. Did you, Dorian?"

"No, Dad," Dorian answered. "I was out like a light. I can't believe this!"

Just then the sheriff walked over, said hello to Chris, and then introduced himself to Bill and Dorian as Jack Donald. Dorian decided to leave the adults to talk and went to find Eric. His first thought was to check the van, but on his way he happened to notice someone sitting on the ground by Victoria all alone.

"Hey, Eric," Dorian said tentatively. "So sorry about Victoria." Getting closer he could see the empty holes in the ground where ancient fossils had laid just yesterday. His heart sank and he said the first thing that came to his mind. "This really sucks!"

"You're telling me!" Eric snapped. "I can't believe someone would stoop so low. It just makes me so angry! All this work for nothing. Dad and the town were counting on this skeleton to draw tourists and investors. We'll never get this museum up and running now! We are running out of time!"

Not knowing what to say in response, Dorian said nothing, but simply walked over and sat beside him on the ground.

"It's probably already overseas by now," Eric continued. "If that's the case, we'll never get it back. We'd have no way to prove it was ours and foreign museums are willing to pay top dollar for articulated dinosaur fossils."

"What about the rest of the bones?" Dorian ventured "Aren't they worth anything?"

"Half a dinosaur is no good to anyone nowadays," Eric replied resignedly.

Pondering Eric's last comment, a thought finally occurred to him. "Well, if the skeleton is not as valuable without the head and front half, then wouldn't the thieves need the rest of it, too?"

Eric took a deep breath and then looked over at Dorian, saying, "You have a good point, but how does that help us?"

Thinking back to the if-then statements used in coding, a plan began to form in his mind. "Logically, this means the thieves will try to come back for the rest of Victoria sometime soon. And, when they do, we can be ready for them. I'm thinking a good old-fashioned stakeout is in order!"

Dinosaurs, Diggers, and Thieves

"I don't think they would have the courage to come back two days in a row," Eric said doubtfully. "But, you may be right. Let's talk to our dads."

After listening to the boys' theory, Tom and Bill agreed. Unfortunately for Dorian and Eric, they also agreed that it would be much too dangerous for two young boys to manage on their own.

"These people could have guns!" Tom warned. "We have no idea who these people are or who they work for. Bill and I will stay here tonight, if that's okay with you Bill?"

"Certainly!" Bill replied. Noticing the disappointed looks on the boys faces, he added, "But, why don't you two camp out by the ranch house tonight. I noticed some old camping gear in a back closet. You could have a bonfire, tell ghost stories, and have a real fun time."

"Good idea, Bill," agreed Tom. "We'll worry about Victoria, and you have a good time close to home."

Both boys knew when they were being talked down to. They also knew it was senseless to argue with either one of their fathers once they had made up their minds about something. No force on heaven or Earth could change it. What their fathers had neglected to recognize, however, was that Dorian and Eric had inherited the same stubborn streak from their dads. They would camp out at the ranch house, all right. But, not to tell ghost stories. They would come up with their own plan to catch the thieves, and it would happen tonight.

Chapter Ten

Dorian found the sky utterly mesmerizing that night. The moon was nothing but a sliver, making the stars shine brighter than he could have ever imagined. This was quite a change from what he was used to in New York City. Yes, he found the sky beautiful, but he also found the darkness that enveloped him a little unnerving. The boys hadn't been able to set up camp until after dark because it had taken a considerable amount of time to convince Susan to sign off on the idea. The fact they would be a mere 400 feet from the house meant little to her.

All three parents had taken turns giving them stern instructions. Bill had made the boys promise to stay close to home and go inside if they saw anyone lurking about. Tom had harped on about fire safety, reminding them to keep a bucket of water nearby and use common sense. Susan had demanded Dorian keep a jacket on and his cell phone on him at all times, even though they both knew it was pretty useless out here.

Once on their own, the boys took the opportunity to vent while gathering kindling to start the fire. "Do they think we are kindergartners or something? Unbelievable!" Dorian complained.

"Yeah, I don't know what they think is going to happen out here. Wasn't it their idea in the first place?"

Soon, the smell of burning wood filled the air. It reminded Dorian of the summer camp he had gone to a few years ago. All around them crickets chirped loudly as they nursed the fire to a healthy glow. Looking back toward the house, Dorian noticed the lights were still on, indicating his mother was still awake. After getting the frustration out of their system, they shifted the conversation to creating a plan for catching the thieves.

"Let's begin by listing the facts," Dorian began.

"Okay," Eric said. "Well, we know the crime took place sometime last night, most likely between the hours of 11:00 p.m. and 4:00 a.m."

"How do you know that?" Dorian questioned.

Dinosaurs, Diggers, and Thieves

"Well, my guess is they wouldn't have risked coming on to your property until after everyone had gone to bed. I took the liberty of asking your parents what time they went to bed while you were packing us some snacks."

Dorian was impressed. Nodding he said, "Makes sense. But, why four in the morning?"

"Well, the sun rises around 6:00 and they would have wanted to be long gone by then. Otherwise, they would risk someone seeing the dust trail from their tires. At the very latest, they would need to leave by 4:30."

"Got it," Dorian agreed. "That seems very logical. We also know there were probably only two thieves, most likely men.

"Now, it's my turn to ask," Eric said. "What makes you think that?"

"Well, I saw only two different sets of shoe prints this morning near the site. One had a diamond pattern on the sole, and the other had circles within circles. Either there were only two people, or more than one person wore the same type of shoe." Dorian took a sip of water from the bottle his mother had given him and then added, "Plus, the shoes looked pretty big and, whoever it was, would need to be pretty strong to lift the fossil."

It was Eric's turn to be impressed. "I like the way you think," he said, smiling over at his new friend. "What else? Oh, we know they drove some type of heavy vehicle. Did you get a look at the tracks?"

"I didn't," Dorian replied. "We will have to take a closer look tomorrow. Maybe take pictures with my phone or something."

"Sounds good. Okay, let's draw a map," Eric said, picking up a stick and starting to draw in the dirt at their feet. "This is the ranch house, and this is the dig site. Now if we—"

AAAAWOOW!

Somewhere in the distance a coyote howled, startling Dorian. "What was that?" he asked, a little shaken up.

"Just a coyote, nothing to worry about," Eric reassured.

This was all new to Dorian. First, there are rattlesnakes, and now there are coyotes? He began to think twice about wanting to sleep outside in a sleeping bag completely accessible to all of nature. He loved animals, but not enough to offer up himself as dinner.

"They're harmless," continued Eric. "I promise!"

Dorian would never admit it, but he was now grateful his mom was only a loud yell away. After a few minutes, Dorian's heart steadied its beating and a peaceful calm came over him again. They continued brainstorming for another ten minutes, but eventually determined they didn't have enough information to do anything until tomorrow.

DINOSAURS TO DRONES

Both boys were secretly relieved and lay back on their sleeping bags to look up at the stars. Dorian had always had a strong interest in constellations and the solar system, but the light pollution in New York City had kept him from seeing the things in real life he studied in his astronomy class last year. Now, he enjoyed pointing out Orion, his favorite constellation, and others he remembered to Eric until they both fell silent.

A bright shooting star streaked across the sky, leaving Dorian almost breathless. "How cool is this!" he whispered to Eric. "Do you ever get a glimpse of the northern lights during the winter time?"

The lack of a response from Eric was a sure sign he had fallen asleep. No doubt the stress of the day's events had taken a toll on him. Just when Dorian was about to close his own eyes, another bright light caught his attention. This light was closer to the horizon and blinked in a steady pattern. It almost looked as if it were a signal of some sort. One thing was for sure: this was no shooting star.

"Eric! Wake up!" Dorian said while shaking his shoulder. "Look! What is that?"

Eric sat up a little dazed and peered in the direction Dorian pointed. The light vanished before Eric could see it. "I said not to worry about those coyotes," he yawned. "We are perfectly safe."

About a minute later a second light began flashing several yards away from the first. "No," Dorian replied. "It's a light. Look over there!"

This time Eric saw it.

"Either there's someone sneaking around out there, or those are the largest lightning bugs I've ever seen," Dorian quipped.

"Our bugs are big in Montana, but not that big," Eric deadpanned.

"Could it possibly be our dads signaling to us?" Dorian wondered aloud.

"I suppose it could be," Eric replied. "Maybe they need our help. I think we should get a closer look."

"Are you sure?" Dorian whispered. "They told us to stay put. And, what about that coyote?"

"Come on, city boy!" Eric teased. "Are you going to wimp out on me?"

"No. Let's just be careful," Dorian said, trying to hide the concern in his voice.

"Follow me!" Eric whispered and then got up and walked toward the mysterious lights.

Just then, a gunshot rang out, stopping both boys in their tracks.

Chapter Eleven

Dorian's heart began to race and he wanted nothing more than to seek shelter inside the house. The thought that his dad might need help, however, spurred him forward. Eric was now almost 20 feet ahead of him and he needed to catch up. It was difficult terrain at the best of times, but in the dead of night without a moon to light the way it was downright unsafe.

Once he managed to close the gap, he took a second to catch his breath and whispered, "Do you see anything?"

"Not yet," Eric replied in a hushed tone. "I'm afraid we still have a long way to go."

"Distances sure can be deceiving out here, can't they?" Dorian asked.

"Shhhh!" Eric admonished. "Let's keep the small talk to a minimum. And, please, can you walk a little quieter? I'm afraid they will hear you coming a mile away."

"I'm sorry," Dorian apologized. "I'm just not used to this terrain yet."

Another 15 minutes into their journey, a second round of flashing lights erupted to their left. This time the lights seemed much closer. After readjusting their course to head in that direction, the boys traveled another 50 yards when, out of the blue, Eric let out a muffled cry and disappeared down an embankment.

Rushing down the hill, Dorian discovered him lying at the bottom gripping his right ankle with both hands. Not sure what to do or say, he asked, "What happened? Are you okay?"

Once Eric could finally answer, it was through gritted teeth. "I'm not sure. Give me a second…My foot got lodged in a rain rut." Judging from the look on his face, the pain must be intense. "I don't think I can move right now. You've got to go on without me."

"Alone?" Dorian asked incredulously. "I'll just get lost, or, or, or make too much noise. There's got to be another way."

"No. There isn't. You can do this," Eric retorted earnestly. "Just go slowly and, for pity's sake, watch out for stupid rain ruts."

DINOSAURS TO DRONES

Realizing Eric was right, Dorian agreed. Before leaving he asked, "Are you sure you will be okay until I get back?"

"I think so," Eric replied. "Now go! There's no time to waste. Our dads might be in great trouble."

Dorian stood up and began to climb the hill he had just climbed down, then stopped to ask a question. "Um, Eric? Are rattlesnakes out at night?"

"Dad told me it's the temperature that determines if they hunt or not. It's mildly chilly, so I doubt it," Eric replied. "Just keep your eyes and ears open! You've got this. Now go!"

Despite feeling extremely apprehensive, he did as Eric ordered. Reaching the top, he took a second to reorient himself. He could see another coulee about a quarter of a mile away and decided to make this his destination. From there, he hoped he would be able to see where to go next. Putting one foot in front of the other, he opened his eyes wide to take in as much light as possible. It was shocking how loud small twigs and pebbles could be when you were trying not to make any noise.

Nearing the summit, he crouched down and took in his surroundings. All he could see from this vantage point was a large boulder on the next rise, about 200 feet up. He took a moment to steady his breath and then crept toward it. As he got closer, however, the boulder began to take shape. It wasn't a boulder at all. No, it was a truck. Hearing voices, he stopped in his tracks and flattened himself against the hill he was climbing.

A deep voice he did not recognize asked, "Did you see something?"

"No," a second voice replied, "but it's so dark. Darn that new moon."

A sudden realization struck Dorian right in the gut. During all of their scheming and brainstorming earlier in the night, they had not talked about what they would do in the event they actually found the thieves. He felt so vulnerable just then, laying on the ground all by himself. Taking a moment to calm himself, he carefully weighed his options. Obviously, there was no way he could capture them alone. But, what could he do? He could get a good look at them and potentially identify them in a police lineup or series of photographs. Checking to make sure the coast was clear, he peeled himself off the wall and continued his climb.

About ten feet from the top, his foot slid on a rock, setting off a small avalanche of smaller stones. If this had been the extent of it, chances are Dorian would have gone undetected. The stones, however, startled a jack rabbit, which sent it leaping away through the surrounding brush, making quite a loud racket.

Dorian's blood froze in his veins as he heard the sound of running feet headed right toward him. Once again, Dorian dropped onto the slanted

Dinosaurs, Diggers, and Thieves

ground where he stood. The man with the deep voice was right above him now, saying gruffly, "What was that?"

Dorian maneuvered his head ever so slightly so he could catch a glimpse of the stranger. Unfortunately, the man's face was engulfed in shadow, but he saw a long, thin object in his hand. A million thoughts ran through his mind. Should he run? If so, in what direction? Should he charge the man while he was off guard? Should he scream? If Eric heard the scream, would he be able to do anything?

Without warning, the man slowly raised the object in his hand and pointed it directly at Dorian. Before he could act, a bright light hit him squarely in the face. The long thin object he was holding wasn't a gun after all. It was just a flashlight! Relief swept over Dorian, but only for a second. He had still been spotted and he was alone out in the middle of nowhere with criminals.

The faceless figure began to walk toward him. Drawing nearer, he lowered the flashlight, allowing Dorian to see his face. It wasn't the face of an international smuggler, but one he had met earlier today – Sheriff Donald. Every muscle in Dorian's body suddenly relaxed.

"You scared me to death!" Dorian gasped.

"Me?" Sheriff Donald scoffed. "You are the one who startled *me*." Then, he reached down to help Dorian climb the remaining few feet.

Looking around, Dorain didn't see anyone else. "So, who were you talking to then?"

"Your father and Tom on my walkie-talkie. But, aren't I the one who is supposed to be asking the questions around here?" the sheriff replied. "Hold on a second while I call them. All I can say is, I wouldn't want to be you right now. Your dad will not be happy when he hears this."

Sheriff Donald radioed the men, who were there in minutes.

Tom was first to speak, asking, "Where's Eric?"

"He's back toward the house. He fell and hurt his ankle, but he's all right."

"You should have stayed put!" Bill scolded. "Who knows what could have happened. He could have hurt a lot more than just his leg, you know."

"I'm sorry, Dad," Dorian replied. "We saw the flashlights and then heard the gunshot. We thought you might have been in trouble."

A confused look overtook Bill's face. "What gunshot? What are you talking about? You must have heard Tom's truck backfire. Was it about half an hour ago?"

Feeling stupid, Dorian nodded his head yes.

"She's old and reliable, but getting crankier all the time," Tom said, shaking his head almost in amusement at the situation.

DINOSAURS TO DRONES

"We had no choice but to call it a night after that. We had given away our position and warned off any would-be prowlers. What were you thinking, son?" Bill scolded.

"What if it *had* been the thieves and they were carrying guns? What would you have done then?" the sheriff asked. "Defend yourselves with sticks and stones?"

Tom mercifully interrupted the lecture by saying, "Please take me to Eric."

Dorian retraced his steps as best he could and managed to lead the small group back to where Eric lay. Tom picked him up and they all walked back to the ranch house. Despite their efforts not to wake Susan, they were predictably unsuccessful. She was a light sleeper in the best of times. Her reaction to what happened was two-fold: (a) give the boys a piece of her mind, and (b) say *"I told you so"* to Tom and Bill.

Honestly speaking, the boys had no good answers for their interrogators that evening. All four adults were correct. They hadn't really thought about the possible consequences. They had just acted out of emotion and a misguided attempt at being heroes. Without protest, they sat quietly and listened to each parent's lecture in turn.

When they ran out of things to say, the sheriff took over. He warned the boys to leave the police work to him and finished by stating, "If only your dinosaur had been located just a few hundred yards to the west. Then it would be on the Bureau of Land Management's property. We could really nail those jerks to the wall then. The punishment for stealing a vertebrate fossil valued at $100 or more is a felony, requiring jail time and steep fines."

Unbeknown to the sheriff, this simple statement inspired an idea that just might lead to the capture of the thieves and the retrieval of the missing skull. It would take courage and persistence, but those were traits neither Dorian nor Eric had in short supply.

Chapter Twelve

The two families made plans the previous night to meet back at the ranch house the next day as close to noon as possible. This would give Tom enough time to check in with the volunteers and have Eric's ankle looked at before heading over. Dorian slept in the next morning until almost 10:30. His parents had decided to let him rest while they busied themselves with the usual tasks associated with moving into a new home.

After washing his face and changing clothes, Dorian headed to the kitchen to find something to eat. Unfortunately, he had to settle for yet another cereal bar because yesterday's unexpected events had prevented the grocery trip into town. Glancing at the clock, he saw he had about an hour to fill before Tom and Eric's arrival. Not one for wasting time, he decided to occupy himself sifting through the mess in the dining room. Yes, his mother would appreciate him chipping in to help, but more importantly, he just might discover a clue or two about his mysterious great-uncle.

Twenty minutes into this task, Susan peaked around the doorframe and greeted him. "Good morning sleepy head! Whatcha doin in here?"

At first, Dorian intended to cover up his ulterior motives, but realized he had an opportunity here. He could continue to let his parents ignore the elephant in the room, or he could be brave. Summoning all his courage, he looked into her eyes and said, "Mom, I'm looking for any shred of information I can find to help fill in the blanks about Uncle Philip. I just can't understand why you and Dad never mentioned him. Even now, when I ask about Philip, you deflect and change the subject."

Susan looked thoughtfully at her son for almost a minute before walking into the room and taking a seat at the old dining room table. Dorian braced himself for the truth and waited patiently for her to speak. Once she did, there was a note of resignation tinged with sadness in her voice. "Well, son, I guess the truth can't be worse than what you must be imagining in your mind. I just need you to promise me something. Promise that you won't think badly of me?"

DINOSAURS TO DRONES

Dorian couldn't even imagine what was going to come next, but he promised her he wouldn't. She smiled weakly at him and then continued on.

"I guess I'll start from the beginning," she said. "Your grandma Mattie, my mother, was seven years older than Philip and practically raised him for the first five years of his life. Up to that point, their childhood had been a happy one, growing up on a farm in Indiana with your great-grandma Freida and great-grandfather Harold. One day, when your grandma Mattie was 13 years old, her father came home from work, packed a suitcase for himself and Philip, then simply drove away. No explanations were given. No apologies made. He just decided he didn't want to be married any longer and left his wife and daughter behind. Sadly, mom wouldn't see her dad or brother for many years to come, but I'll get to that in a minute."

Dorian didn't have any siblings, but understood how devastating that must have been. It had been hard enough leaving his friends behind in New York City.

"About a year after the divorce was finalized," she continued, "Freida eventually remarried. It was hard for women who already had children to find husbands in those days, and so she felt as if she couldn't be too selective. Unfortunately, your grandma's new stepfather was not very kind to either of them. He was a gruff man and had no business raising children. Once Grandma Mattie was old enough to marry and have a family of her own, she met your grandpa Ezra, fell in love, and had me."

"What year was that, Mom?" Dorian inquired.

"I was born in 1978," she clarified.

Dorian followed up by asking, "Didn't Philip and Mattie try to contact each other after they were separated?"

"Well, Mom didn't know where her father and brother had ended up settling down; and remember, there wasn't an internet in those days to help locate them. Philip had been so young at the time, I doubt he even would have known how to go about it. Anyway, when I was two, Harold did finally reach out to her, hoping to reconnect with the daughter he had abandoned all those years ago. Mom was leery about the whole thing, but decided to give him a chance. I think what swayed her was the recognition that this would allow her to see her beloved brother again as well."

"What did Great-Grandma Freida think about this whole thing?" Dorian interrupted.

"Surprisingly, she was happy for mom and told her she should do what she thought best. She just didn't want to hear all the details. During Mom's first planned meetup with her long-lost father, she was surprised to discover Harold had remarried and she now had two half sisters and a half brother she had never met. Philip was there also and the two of them had a beautiful, tearful reunion. Harold, Philip, and your grandma visited each other about once a month for the next three years. Mom really felt as if a missing piece in her life had finally been filled…I need a glass of water, honey. I'll be right back."

Susan stood up and left the room, leaving Dorian to ponder all he had heard. This was not at all what he had expected. So far, the story was very sad, but a little anticlimactic. A few minutes later, she returned, carrying a glass of water for each of them. Eager to know more, he prompted her to begin again by saying, "So, I still don't understand how Philip became a big family secret, or why you would think I would ever be disappointed in you. There's got to be more to the story than this!"

"Indeed there is," she proclaimed. "On my fifth birthday, Mom decided to drive me over to visit Harold and Philip. As soon as we pulled into the driveway, we knew something was wrong. The house appeared to be completely empty and there was a For Sale sign in the yard. Believe it or not, Harold had abandoned her for a second time, leaving no word where he and his new family had gone. You have no idea how hurt she was! Mom was even more hurt this time because Philip was old enough to speak up and at least call to say goodbye. Three or four years later, Philip did finally contact your grandma. He called to tell her that Harold had just passed away from a heart attack. During this conversation he also tried to explain why he hadn't reached out until now, but Mom refused to listen. She thanked him for letting her know about her father and then asked him never to contact her again, before hanging up the phone. From that point on, she refused to talk about anyone from that side of the family again."

Dorian's heart hurt for his grandma. "I just feel so bad for her," he said once his mind wrapped around this revelation. "How could anyone do that to one of their own children? She must have felt so betrayed, especially since her father had three new children, two of which were girls like her. He raised them, but left her behind like she was nothing."

"I know, honey. There's no excuse for what happened. When mom passed away a few years back, Philip somehow found out. I guess he had been keeping tabs on her all along. He sent me a heartfelt letter saying how sorry he was for not trying harder to be a part of Mom's life and hoped he and I could still have a relationship one day. Deep down, I blamed Harold for all the hurt that was caused, not Philip, but I never responded. I just kept thinking, 'Maybe one day.' But, now, I guess, I waited too long. I really regret that now and will probably never forgive myself."

Dorian could hear the sadness and sincerity in her words and reached out to comfort her with a hug. Letting go, Dorian realized he had one more question. "But, why do you think he left the ranch to you when you weren't even on speaking terms?"

"From what I understand from your uncle's lawyer, he never married and didn't have any children of his own. I guess this was his final attempt at making things right between us. There's nothing I can do to change the past, but I'm glad we have the opportunity to get to know him through his friends here in Saddle Creek and to help the town he loved so much."

A single tear slid down her cheek. Dorian hated to see his mother cry.

For the second time, Susan looked her son square in the eyes. "I want you to always be able to talk to me about anything. Your grandmother was a wonderful person and a good mom, but we never talked about our feelings. I don't want that to happen to us. Okay, son?"

"Okay, Mom. I promise."

After another long hug, Susan stood up and said, "Well, have fun looking through all this stuff. Just don't make it even messier than it already is."

As she turned to leave, Dorian stopped her by saying, "Mom? I love you."

"I love you too, honey! More than you know." After blowing him a kiss, she left Dorian alone with his thoughts.

Dorian spent the next hour and a half in the dining room scouring through all the files and folders that covered almost every surface. Nearing the bottom of a particularly tall stack of papers, an old map caught his attention. It was different from those hanging on the walls. Studying it carefully, an idea began to form in his mind. It was definitely worth talking over with Eric when he arrived.

As if on cue, Eric hobbled into the dining room on a single crutch and greeted Dorian with a robust, "Hey there!"

"Hi!" Dorian returned warmly without looking up from the map. "I didn't hear the truck pull up. I was just going through all this stuff and I found something I want to show you. I've been thinking about what the sheriff said last night and I might have an idea to help get Victoria back. All we have to do is…"

Finally peeling his eyes from the map, he looked at Eric and saw the crutch for the first time. A disappointing reality registered in his mind. They could not carry out his potential idea if one of the most valuable players on the team was on the disabled list. He let the map he had been studying fall back to the table, exclaiming, "Noooo! Are you okay? I should have asked right away."

"I'm fine," Eric replied. "It's just a bad sprain, but I have to use this for a while. What were you saying about an idea?"

Dinosaurs, Diggers, and Thieves

With far less enthusiasm in his voice, Dorian explained, "Well, I had a plan to talk over with you, but I need two sets of legs to make it work. It's not your fault, of course, but I guess we will have to let our dads have the fun. What a bummer! But, the important part is we catch those no-good jerks."

Eric interrupted him, saying, "Slow down! What are you talking about? Where there is a will, there is a way. Tell me what you're thinking."

Dorian explained his idea step by step.

"This is actually doable," Eric exclaimed. "I may not be able to help the way I want, but I know some people who can."

Dorian wondered aloud, "Who do you mean?"

"Zade, Sylvia, and Jose, of course. Plus, we have your nifty drone to assist us as well."

The idea of enlisting the volunteers had never occurred to him. "But, will they do it?" Dorian asked. "Can we trust them?"

"Well, there's only one way to find out," Eric said. "We'll talk to them tomorrow."

Chapter Thirteen

Monday morning everyone assembled at the dig site once more. Sheriff Donald had given Tom the go-ahead the previous evening after explaining all the evidence that could be collected had been. Alexander, already in a bad mood, exited the van complaining loudly that "Only a dingbat would leave a dinosaur skeleton unprotected overnight."

Tom just sighed and began to divide the group in half. Due to Eric's injured ankle, he would oversee the work on Victoria today and Tom would lead the scouting party. Those going with Tom included Cassandra, Alexander, and a well-rested Sylvia. That left Jose, Zade, and Dorian to assist Eric. Dorian couldn't be happier, for two reasons: (1) he wouldn't have to put up with the twins, and (2) he would have the perfect opportunity to potentially recruit two of the three volunteers they would need to help with his new master plan.

Cassandra, never one to be outdone by her brother in the sarcasm department, asked before leaving with the scouting group, "Is it safe to leave my camera behind, or will someone steal that too?"

Eric was the first to respond. "Well, you can take your pick. Leave it here or risk one of those horrible horned toads you love so much swallowing it." His comment had the desired effect, for she stormed off in a huff, mumbling something unintelligible under her breath.

"All right men," Tom said to Eric, Dorian, Jose, and Zade. "I'm counting on you to take care of my girl while I'm away. She no longer has a head and half of her is missing, but it could have been much worse. Zade? You and Dorian get those brushes over there and carefully remove the dirt covering that bone right there. Remember, don't use much force. This is fragile material. Be gentle and use light strokes."

Eric, who was seated on a lawn chair with his leg propped up on a cooler, reminded his father, "You can trust me. I've only seen you orchestrate a dig like, oh, I don't know, three hundred times!"

Dinosaurs, Diggers, and Thieves

"You know what?" Tom replied. "You are right! I'll shut up and let the four of you get to work. See you at lunch time, gang."

"Finally!" Eric said once the scouting group headed down the side of the hill. He loved his dad, but felt like he deserved a little more trust after the ten-year apprenticeship he had enjoyed working side by side with his father. This thought reminded him of what his mother used to say. "You practically cut your teeth on dinosaur bones as a toddler." Oh, how he missed his mother. Eric knew he couldn't dwell on these thoughts for long, so he pulled himself together and announced, "You heard the man. Let's get this show on the road."

Zade handed Dorian a brush and then demonstrated the proper technique Tom had taught him only a few days ago. After a few minutes of working in silence, Dorian cleared his throat and tried to make small talk with him, saying, "So Zade, you're from Chicago? What's that like?"

"It's okay," he said, but nothing more.

Dorian realized this was going to be harder than he thought. He couldn't quite tell if Zade was shy, antisocial, or simply focused. Trying again, Dorian said, "I'm from New York City. Have you ever been there?"

Again, Zade's reply was short and sweet. "Nope."

Undaunted, Dorian pushed onward. "Have you enjoyed working on the dig so far?"

"Yes," he replied, offering no more information than necessary.

Feeling frustrated, Dorian replied before he could stop himself. "Don't talk much, do ya?"

"No, I don't," Zade answered, looking up from the ground for the first time. His tone was direct, but not angry or unkind. "Don't have time to either. I want to be a paleontologist and the only way to do that is to go to college. If I'm going to college, I have to have a scholarship because, Lord knows, my mother can't afford it. To get a scholarship I need to study, work hard, and have excellent recommendations like the one I hope to get from Tom. That doesn't leave much time for idle chitchat, now does it?"

A little taken aback by the sudden flood of words aimed in his direction, Dorian regrouped and said, "No. I guess not." He respected determination in people, and Zade seemed set on making his dream of becoming a paleontologist come true.

For a long while, Dorian worked earnestly on Victoria without uttering another word. He occupied himself by listening to the conversation taking place between Jose and Eric instead. Jose seemed to be the exact opposite of Zade, for he had been prattling on now for almost 20 minutes about how he didn't believe all the dinosaurs were actually extinct.

"And, I have proof," Jose promised. "My close friend was in the Congo while in Africa and saw a huge reptile that he swears could have been a dinosaur. He didn't get a picture or anything, but I know he's telling the truth. Well, he wasn't a close friend exactly. He was just someone I met at a party one time. He seemed trustworthy, though, not loco at all. Wait a minute. Did he say he read about it online or did he see it himself? I don't remember. The point is someone saw it, right?"

The look on Eric's face said it all. He could tell Eric couldn't wait for Jose to stop rambling and regretted he was confined to that chair. Dorian wondered how Eric's annoyance could be so obvious to everyone else, yet Jose couldn't see it. Thinking back to some of the people he used to go to school with, he answered his own question. For whatever reason, some people were just oblivious.

At this point, Zade mumbled something under his breath.

"What was that?" inquired Dorian.

"Nothing," he whispered. "It's just, do you believe this guy? Everyone knows dinosaurs went extinct 65 million years ago. If I have to listen to any more of his quack ideas about Loch Ness or Bigfoot, I just might scream!"

Dorian couldn't imagine Zade screaming. He had barely said ten words to him the whole morning. "He's getting on your nerves too, huh?"

Zade nodded vigorously, then said, "He's my roommate back at the hotel and all he wants to talk about are his theories on how to catch a leprechaun, why he is sure mermaids really existed, and the friend who personally saw a fairy once. Next thing you know, he'll be saying he's going to wait in the pumpkin patch this Halloween with Linus for the Great Pumpkin to arrive!"

Dorian laughed and could tell he was going to like Zade after all. He wasn't rude or antisocial. He was just a serious intellectual that didn't have time for small talk. He was even quite funny once you got to know him.

Periodically throughout the day, Dorian and Zade talked about a multitude of subjects. Dorian always let him be the first to speak because he didn't want to break his concentration. Eventually, while Eric was stuck in another long, drawn-out conversation with Jose, Dorian got up the nerve to bring up his idea. Fortunately, it didn't take much to convince Zade to agree to be part of the mission. He did have one stipulation, however. It could in no way jeopardize his chances at getting a stellar letter of recommendation from Tom.

Next came the harder task. How could he get Jose to stop talking long enough to listen to what he had to say. Thinking carefully, Dorian Realized he could use Jose's gift for gab to his advantage. As soon as Eric began to walk Zade through the proper way to put a plaster jacket on Victoria's remaining radius and ulna, Dorian approached Jose.

Dinosaurs, Diggers, and Thieves

"So, I couldn't help overhearing you talking about dinosaurs in the Congo. That's cool!"

"Yes it is," he replied. "The natives call it *mokele-mbembe*. It was first documented in 1873. It has a huge long neck, a small head, and leaves giant footprints on the forest floor. The name means 'one who stops the flow of rivers.'"

Dorian acted interested and nodded along politely. He would just have to bide his time until Jose took a drink of water or exhausted himself. Finally, about ten minutes later, he found his opportunity.

"That's just fascinating," he said. Secretly, Dorian had to admit that it really was pretty interesting. How amazing would it be if there really were dinosaurs still alive somewhere on Earth! Knowing he didn't have time to beat around the bush, Dorian quickly blurted out, "So, I have a question for you. What if I told you that Eric and I have a plan to catch the people who stole Victoria? It's very hush-hush so you wouldn't be able to tell anyone about it."

Without so much as a pause, Jose said, "You came to the right person. You bet I can keep a secret! I've kept the fact I saw an alien once a secret for seven years. It told me not to tell a living soul and I never have. Well, oops, I guess until today, that is." Jose then proceeded to look up into the sky and say, "Lo siento!"

Trying not to laugh, Dorian replied, "I'll give you the details later, but the main thing we need you to do is do what you do best."

"What's that?" Jose inquired.

"Talk! Talk about cryptozoology with Bill and Tom Thursday night. We'll need you to keep them preoccupied and away from their radios. It will all make sense later. Can you do that?"

"Can I talk? You bet. I can tell them about the thunderbirds, the Kraken, the Sirrush, or even the Ogopogo. Wait! Are you going to be careful, mijo? I wouldn't want anyone to get hurt or anything."

"Yes," Dorian reassured him. "No worries in that department. I think we learned our lesson the other night. Oh, one more question. Can I borrow your GPS unit you carry with you? I'll be really careful with it."

"Sure," Jose offered.

"Thanks," he replied, and then out of curiosity asked, "So, what are thunderbirds?"

Chapter Fourteen

That evening, Eric called Dorian on Philip's landline to tell him about a conversation he had with Sylvia that night at dinner. Evidently, the volunteers ate with Tom and Eric every night at Skinny Joe's Pizza or the hotel dining room while planning for the next day. The old-fashioned rotary dial phone felt clunky in Dorian's hand and he missed the smooth, light feel of his now almost-useless smartphone.

"I'll start with the good news," Eric began. "As we both expected, Sylvia is willing to help in any way she can. She also said that this reminded her of the days she served as a spy for a former president she refused to name. If it were anyone other than Sylvia, I would have laughed, thinking it was a joke."

Fascinated, Dorian made a mental note to ask Sylvia about this later, then said, "Now, do I want to hear the bad news?"

"Probably not, but here goes. Cassandra and Alexander kind of overheard me talking to Sylvia."

Before Eric could say anything more, Dorian interrupted. "What? You've got to be kidding me!"

"You know how sneaky they are," Eric said defensively. "They threatened to tell Dad and everything."

"Probably for no other reason than spite, I'm sure," Dorian guessed.

"Who knows, but don't worry. I dealt with it," Eric reassured.

"How?" Dorian mused.

With a note of sadness in his voice, Eric said, "Well, they kind of bribed me."

"What do you mean they bribed you?" asked Dorian.

"In exchange for not blowing the whistle, I had to promise them two things. The first thing they wanted was my tyrannosaur tooth."

"No way!" Dorian exclaimed. "You can't give them that. You love that tooth!"

Dinosaurs, Diggers, and Thieves

"It was the only thing that would close the deal. That, and…I had to promise they could help with the plan."

"You've got to be kidding me," Dorian quipped. "You wouldn't seriously trust them with something this important, would you? You know we only really have one shot at this, right?"

"I know, but they didn't give me much of a choice. It was either say 'yes,' hope for the best, and stand a chance at succeeding, or say 'no' and it would be over before we even started." After a pause, Eric added, "I know I give them a hard time, but they aren't totally useless."

"Oh really?" Dorian said sarcastically. "Since when?"

"Since their rich father agreed to pay a security guard to patrol the dig site every night from 11:00 p.m. to 7:00 a.m. Evidently, they complained so much to their father about the theft ruining their time that he called Dad last night and made the arrangements. Did you know our dads were planning on camping out there every night for at least the next week or two?" Eric asked.

"No," Dorian replied, "but I kind of expected they might. I guess the twins' whining does come in handy sometimes. Let's say we do let them help. What are they going to do anyway?"

"Well," Eric began, "you and I need to go back to the drawing board and take them into consideration. I know we can make this work, but it's not going to be easy. We have a little bit of time, at least. Step one of the plan still remains unchanged."

"True," Dorian answered. "But, we need to move forward with step one as soon as possible. Let's call it 'Operation Rumor Mill.'"

Early the next day, Dorian and Eric filled their fellow conspirators in on the details of step one. Simply put, they would need to spread false information around town that a new amazing dinosaur fossil had been discovered at Cretaceous Ranch. That was easy enough, but the tricky part was making sure the fake news didn't get back to Tom, Bill, or Susan.

"We will need to make everyone we share this false information with thinks it is a secret entrusted only to them," Dorian explained.

"Plus," Eric added. "Dad is going to be so busy following up on leads and digging up the rest of her that he probably won't come into town much anyway."

"What about our nightly planning sessions at dinner?" Zade asked.

"You'll just have to be super careful," Dorian stressed. "We'll need you, Jose, to talk Tom's ear off. Also, Cassandra and Alexander, if someone we've spoken to approaches Dad at all, can you two create a distraction by getting into a fight or something?"

All three agreed.

"What are we supposed to tell everyone, exactly?" Sylvia inquired.

"Tell them that we've made a once-in-a-lifetime find. Tell them that we've found a never-before-seen theropod," instructed Eric.

"And, that it is located on the western-most portion of the ranch, about half a mile off the road," Dorian added. "The location is very important! Tell them it is where a stream empties into a small pond."

"If we play our cards right, everyone in the town will know by sunset tomorrow. Especially if you tell Roxanne. She will make it her duty to tell everyone she sees. People in this town can't sneeze without her knowing about it," joked Eric.

"That's all we have to do?" Sylvia asked.

"For now," answered Eric. "We'll tell you the rest of the plan tomorrow. We have a few last-minute details to iron out first. Right now, focus on spreading the word. Can you do that when you get back in town tonight for dinner, everyone?"

"Yeah, just don't forget your promise about that tooth," muttered Alexander.

Before Eric could reply, Cassandra growled, "And what will you two lazy bums be doing while we're doing all the dirty work?"

The boys simply looked at each other and smiled. While the others were in town that evening for dinner, they would be on a mission of their own.

Chapter Fifteen

The map Dorian had found in the dining room had revealed exactly where Cretaceous Ranch stopped and federal land began. The dotted lines marking the boundaries on the yellowed document were easy to see, but in the real world, the borders would be much more difficult to delineate. On the plus side, this would make it possible for Dorian and Eric to trick the thieves into trespassing on and stealing from government property. On the negative side, it would be possible for Dorian and Eric to make a mistake. If they misread the map, it could mean the thieves getting nothing more than a slap on the wrist instead of jail time and huge fines.

Keeping all this in mind, the boys chose their search area carefully. The easiest place to identify on the map, geographically speaking, had been where a small stream and pond meet, about three miles from the ranch house. Eric's injury prevented him from taking the journey himself; so it would be up to Dorian alone to find the stream, follow it to the pond, and then locate a worthwhile fossil, all in the next few hours.

"And, it can't be a piece of chuck-a-saurus either," Eric reminded him. "It has to be large enough for the government to want to prosecute those jerks."

"You know I'm just an amateur, right?" Dorian said. "I've barely had two days of training. This is going to be harder than finding a needle in a haystack."

"Yeah, I know," Eric replied. "And, I hate to mention this, but you only have a couple more hours of daylight. You know your parents will get suspicious if you're not back before dark."

"Thanks for pointing that out. I feel so much better now," Dorian said sarcastically.

"Sorry, man," added Eric. "Where did you tell them you were going anyway?"

"Just to play around with the radios your dad said we could borrow."

Eric then took his backpack off his shoulder, dug around until he found them, and then gave one to Dorian and kept one for himself.

"I will really need your help!" Dorian pleaded. "If I pick up something I think is a fossil and it turns out not to be? Well, you know what that means."

"You can do this!" Eric assured him. "I have faith in you. Just remember to look for that unique pattern I showed you and don't forget about the tongue test. We'll be fine as long as you don't pick up another rabbit bone."

"Very funny!" Dorian sneered. "Did you also bring Jose's GPS unit with you like we talked about? I'll use it to mark the spot where the fossil is so we can give the exact coordinates to the police when the time comes."

"Yes. Here it is," Eric said, handing Dorian the device. "Call me as soon as you find anything!"

"Will do!" Dorian promised, and then started walking away.

In a matter of minutes, Dorian reached the summit of the nearest hill. Checking the built-in compass on the GPS unit, he noted the fact he was heading due west. He was on target and should reach the stream in about 20 to 30 minutes. So many thoughts ran through his mind as he walked. Was this whole thing just wishful thinking? Were they being naive? What really were the chances that an inexperienced novice from New York City would find a fossil out in the middle of nowhere by himself? The only thing keeping him from turning around and heading back in defeat was the sad look Dorian had seen on Eric's face when he found out a part of Victoria had been stolen. He might not be successful, but he made up his mind to at least try.

Thirty-five minutes later, Dorian still hadn't spotted the waterway. Speaking loudly and clearly into the radio, he asked, "Eric? Are you there? Over."

Almost instantly, Eric replied, "This is Eric. Found anything yet? Over."

"No. I can't even find the stream."

"Wish I could help, man," Eric said. "Stupid ankle!"

"Don't beat yourself up. I know you'd help if you could," Dorian replied.

"Just keep going," Eric encouraged. "You've got to be close now."

With each passing moment the sun slipped closer to the horizon. Dorian trudged forward over hills, through valleys, and around cliffs. He could see nothing that even remotely looked like a stream. His stomach growled and he began to feel thirsty. At least he had the GPS unit with him. If he got lost he would be able to retrace his steps in order to get home.

Fifteen minutes later, Eric called back to check on Dorian's progress. "Dorian. This is Eric. Over."

Dinosaurs, Diggers, and Thieves

"This is Dorian."

"What's the status? Any luck?" he inquired.

Dorian's lack of a response told him all he needed to know. Trying hard to keep the disappointment out of his voice, Eric said, "It's getting late. You'll have to think about heading back soon. We'll just have to search again tomorrow."

Dorian was stubborn and didn't want to give up. "Not yet. Just a few more minutes."

After looking at the map for the hundredth time and checking the compass on the GPS unit, he peered out into the distance. He saw nothing that looked remotely like a stream or pond. Glancing at his watch, Dorian estimated he had about an hour of sunlight left. It would take him about that long just to get home. Making up his mind to climb one more hill before calling it a day, Dorian began climbing.

Reaching the top, he was met with a beautiful sight. The golden rays of the sun pierced through and around the few clouds in the sky, casting long shadows on the ground. Sadly, there was no stream in sight and he was out of time. He didn't want to turn back, but he also didn't like the thought of being out here alone in the dark. Regretfully, he resigned himself to heading back.

Just then, something caught his eye. The dying light was reflecting off something just below him. Walking closer, he realized there was a tiny, almost nonexistent creek about ten yards away. He probably would have missed it if the angle of the sun had been any different. Could this be it? Maybe the stream mostly dried up during the summer. It was possible, but where was the pond?

Leaping down the hill, he stepped over the rivulet of water and then followed it north toward the road in the distance. His hopes began to rise. Walking another five minutes, he rounded a corner and there, before his eyes, was a pond about the size of a child's swimming pool. It had looked much larger on the map, but just like the stream, it had mostly dried up.

His first order of business was to mark its location using the global positioning system. Next, he knelt down, took the backpack off his shoulder and pulled out a hand trowel, a pick, and a brush. He quickly set to work turning over the dirt so that it would resemble an active dig site. His hole was only a few inches deep, but spanned almost three feet in diameter once he was finished.

Realizing he still had not called Eric, he paused and pushed the call button on the radio.

"Eric, this is Dorian. Over."

"This is Eric. Are you on your way back? Over."

DINOSAURS TO DRONES

"No, but I found the pond!" Dorian said excitedly. "It's smaller than we thought, but I found it! I just need to find a bone now."

"There's no time!" Eric insisted. "You've got to get back here. Your mom just hollered over to say supper would be ready in half an hour."

"Cover for me. Tell her anything, but I need a little bit more time. I can do this! I know it!" Dorian insisted.

"I'll try!" Eric replied.

Putting down the radio, Dorian frantically began searching the ground in front of him. Remembering what Sylvia had said about walking quickly to find large fossils and slowly for small fossils, he charged forward. The sun was beginning to go behind the horizon line so Dorian knew he had, at the most, 15 minutes. Four minutes later, he came across a section of land on the side of a coulee that resembled a small landslide.

Thinking this might be a good place to search, Dorian stepped around a medium-sized shrub on his way to see what might be poking out of the exposed dirt. Doing this disturbed a beautiful butterfly that had been perched on one of its branches. He stopped just long enough to watch until it landed on something white laying on the ground near the main stem of the bush. Bending over to examine what it was, he realized what he was looking at. It was a bone about a foot and a half long. His heart began pounding in his chest as he carefully picked it up to examine more thoroughly.

It had the same spongy pattern he remembered from before. In fact, it looked almost exactly like the radius he had helped Eric with just yesterday. If he had more time, he would have loved to follow the bone trail, but he'd have to wait for another day to do that. The sun was no longer visible in the sky and he had one more thing to do. Dorian ran toward the hole he had made near the pond and placed the bone carefully in the dirt. He was out of breath and thirstier than ever, but his heart soared with joy. He had done it!

Chapter Sixteen

Everything was falling into place. The twins had spread the word at the general store and Skinny Joe's Pizza, Jose and Sylvia had "accidentally" been overhead discussing it at the post office and train station, and Zade had gotten the attention of the most crucial target of all, Saddle Creek's biggest gossip, Roxanne.

He had found her inside Martha's on Main, the only clothing store in town, chatting away with the owner. Both women stopped talking instantly when they saw who had entered the store.

Quite naturally, this made Zade very uncomfortable, not knowing if they were reacting to his skin color or to the fact that he was a stranger.

Deciding not to jump to conclusions, he approached the women and greeted them politely. "Hello, ladies! I'm Zade. It's nice to meet you. I'm here working with Tom and just wanted to stop by to see if I could find a nice thank-you gift for my mother. You see, it was because of her that I was able to come on this trip."

This had been the perfect thing to say. Both women seemed to relax immediately and helped him find a beautiful scarf in his price range. While Martha went into the back room to find a nice gift box for it, Roxanne casually asked how things were going at the dig site.

Thinking on his feet, Zade replied, "Which one?"

A confused look blanketed her face a full ten seconds before she replied saying, "What do you mean 'which one'? Isn't there only one dinosaur?"

Pretending to realize he had made a mistake, Zade covered his mouth and said, "Please pretend I didn't just say that! I wasn't supposed to say anything yet, and I don't want to lose my scholarship."

Sensing an opportunity to learn a new juicy piece of gossip, Roxanne put on her sweetest smile and said, "I wouldn't dream of telling Tom about your little slip of the tongue. You can trust me. I'm known around here as someone people can confide in. My word is my bond!"

DINOSAURS TO DRONES

Inside his mind, Zade was laughing. He knew what she was known for and it wasn't keeping secrets. After filling her in about the exact location of the "new theropod," he bid her a good afternoon and walked out of the store with a wide smile plastered on his face.

Over lunch the next day, Dorian and Eric explained the next piece of the plan.

"We need everyone to meet at my house tomorrow night at 7:00 p.m.," Dorian instructed. With a jolt, he realized this was the first time he had used the word *my* when referring to his uncle's ranch house. Surprisingly, it did not feel as foreign as he thought it would.

"I've told Dad that you all want to do some stargazing and Dorian is going to point out a few constellations," Eric continued.

"Dad and Tom will be guarding Victoria at the dig site until the night watchmen arrive, so this will give us about three hours to work with," Dorian explained. "But, just to be sure, will you volunteer to assist them, Jose, and then talk their ears off like we discussed?"

"Sure, amigo! Anything to help the cause," he replied.

"Ummm, that's not all we need you to do," Eric added and then paused dramatically.

Now apprehensive, Jose prodded him, saying, "Continue, por favor!"

"Well," Dorian began, "We sort of, kind of, need you to sneakily turn off Tom's handheld radio when he's not looking."

"Are you two loco?" Jose exclaimed, looking back and forth between the two boys. "How am I supposed to do that? You know he keeps it clipped to his belt whenever we are out in the field."

"True," Eric replied. "It's not going to be easy, but can't you just call on the spirit of some invisible mantis creature, or ask a skinwalker for help?"

"Ha ha, mijo," Jose responded in a humorless tone, crossing his arms. "It's about time you all show a little more respect for what I do."

Jose's reaction surprised everyone. Mild-mannered Jose had never reacted this way before to the teasing he received by the others.

Feeling chagrined about his comment, Eric said, "You know what, Jose? You are right. I'm sorry if I was disrespectful. I guess because my dad is a scientist, I don't believe in all that Bigfoot, Loch Ness mumbo jumbo. That's not an excuse, though. Will you forgive me?"

After a few seconds of contemplation, a smile returned to Jose's face and he thrust his hand out for Eric to shake. "Of course I do! Water under the bridge."

Seizing the opportunity to change the subject, Dorian cleared his throat and said, "Cassandra, we'll need you to bring your camera tomorrow, flash included. Can you do that? It will be important for us to have concrete proof and take a picture of those bozos in action."

"I guess," Cassandra said, shrugging dismissively.

Dinosaurs, Diggers, and Thieves

"And Alexander," Eric added, "we need you to spend some of that allowance you've mentioned a few times to some of us."

"What?" Alexander yelled. "I only get $75 a week!"

Staying calm, Eric stated, "Well, the choice is yours, but, uh, if you want that tooth, I'd strongly suggest you pony up the money."

"You wish!" Alexander said mockingly, but was clearly mulling it over in his mind. They waited patiently for his verdict, which did not disappoint. "Fine. What am I buying anyway?"

"We need you to purchase another set of radios," Dorian answered. "A set similar to the one Tom uses."

"Why?" Alexander barked. "Those have to be a couple hundred dollars!"

"We will need you to contact Eric, who will be stationed at the ranch house with my mom, as soon as the thieves have struck. Eric will then phone the police."

Dorian took Alexander's lack of a response as a yes.

"What's Zade going to do in all this?" Cassandra whined. "Why is he getting off so easily? Shouldn't he have to do my job for me since my father is the one who paid for him to be here in the first place?"

Dorian had to bite his tongue to keep from lashing out at her. Luckily, Eric did it for him. "You better shut your mouth! If you say one more word, I'll find a horned toad or two and make sure they find a nice warm place to sleep tonight. Oh, I don't know, your bed would do nicely!"

It was this comment and the expression of rage on Sylvia's face that led to a minor miracle taking place. Cassandra actually asked for forgiveness. Zade, who had remained stoic, simply raised his head and nodded one curt yes in Cassandra's general direction. Dorian could tell he was used to ignorant people like Cassandra, but he would love to see Zade let her have it one day.

"Anyway, back to what I was saying," Dorian continued. "Zade will be stationed back near the main road, where he will be responsible for leading the police to where the thieves are. We will give you the GPS coordinates, so it should be easy."

"No problem," Zade responded.

"And me?" asked Sylvia eagerly. "Where will I be?"

"You probably have the most difficult job of all," Eric said. "You will be tasked with making sure Cassandra and Alexander don't kill each other."

A look of pure glee filled Sylvia's face. "You know I'm a black belt in karate, right? One word out of these two and..." then she spun around and took an attack pose just a few feet from where the twins were standing. The looks on their faces were priceless. Everyone, except for Cassandra and Alexander, cheered and clapped at what they had just seen.

Chapter Seventeen

At 7:03 p.m., a van full of nervously excited conspirators pulled up to the ranch house. Tom, who had driven out separately about an hour earlier, was just heading to his truck with Bill in tow when they arrived. Seeing his work crew pull up, Tom greeted them warmly. "Have a good time guys, but don't stay out too late. We've got a lot of work to do tomorrow."

"Promise, Dad," Eric said to his father as he hobbled up to the front door of the ranch house, where he would be spending the evening playing cards with Susan.

Jose, seizing his one and only opportunity to fulfill his portion of the mission, ran over to Tom, saying, "Can I tag along? There is something I have been meaning to talk to you about."

Without a good excuse for turning him away, Tom made the only argument he could think of. "But, you don't want to miss the stargazing, do you?"

In order to ensure Tom had no reason to suspect anything, Dorian chimed in saying, "Yeah, Jose. I'm going to point out Proxima Centauri, then Rigil Kentaurus right over there, and Sirius B right near the horizon there. You're going to miss all the fun!"

"Not this time, guys," Jose replied, playing his part well. "I've got some theories to talk over with your dad." Then, shifting his attention back to Tom, he said, "You sure are a busy man. I can't even get uno momento to chat. Seems like we get interrupted every time. Tonight will be the perfect chance to talk without any distractions. Qué bueno?"

"Sure. No problem," Tom said resignedly. Waving goodbye, the three men got into the truck and drove away.

As soon as they were out of sight, Alexander handed Eric the new radio he had purchased, along with a stern warning, "And don't break it!"

In response, Eric tossed it from hand to hand before pretending to drop it. He caught it before it hit the ground and teased, "Oops! I guess

Dinosaurs, Diggers, and Thieves

I'll have to be more careful." If looks could kill, Eric would have died right there on the spot.

"Oh, that reminds me," Dorian said. "You have your camera with you, right, Cassandra?"

The wide-eyed look on her face told everyone that she didn't. Comprehension now dawning on her, she said defensively, "I forgot, okay? You should have reminded me sooner. People make mistakes, you know!"

Alexander glared at her in disbelief and said, "It's probably because you were staring in that mirror so long trying to look good for *you-know-who*."

This statement piqued everyone's curiosity. There were only three boys even remotely Cassandra's age on this trip, not counting her brother, so it shouldn't be too difficult to deduce who the object of her affection might be. All Dorian knew was that he hoped and prayed it wasn't him.

Susan, unaware of what was going on, walked out onto the front porch to greet everyone and added fuel to the fire by asking, "Who is *you-know-who*?"

Not one to pass up a chance to embarrass his sister, Alexander gleefully responded, "Dorian, of course. She can't stand Eric or Zade."

Within a split second, three things happened at once. Cassandra kicked her brother in the shins, Eric burst out laughing, and Dorian turned bright red in embarrassment. Cassandra's rage was quickly replaced with horror and she covered her face and wept.

Dorian felt sorry for her, but did not know how to help. It was times like these he was glad he didn't have a sibling. Sylvia, on the other hand, knew exactly what to do. She wasted no time in verbally throttling Alexander for disrespecting his sister and attempted to comfort Cassandra with a hug. Looking for any opportunity to escape the awkwardness of the moment, Dorian and Eric snuck inside.

"Don't even say a word," Dorian commanded.

Knowing he meant business, Eric resisted the urge to make a wisecrack and said, "Okay, okay. I'll keep it focused on the problem at hand. What are we going to do now without her camera? We need photographic evidence to put these guys away."

"I know," Dorian responded. Finding it hard to think with all the shouting and crying going on right outside the front door, he led Eric back to his bedroom.

Just inside his room, an idea struck him like a ton of bricks. The answer was right there on his dresser. They would use his drone.

Fifteen minutes later, when everyone had calmed down, Sylvia, Cassandra, Alexander, and Zade fell into line behind Dorian and headed toward the faux dig site. Once out of earshot of the ranch house, Dorian looked over his shoulder and said, "Everyone knows what to do when we get there, right?"

Perhaps in an effort to prove just how little she liked Dorian after all, Cassandra snapped back, "You don't have to keep repeating the plan over and over again. Eric already did that a dozen times in the van on the way over here. Do you think we are all morons or something?"

"Well, if the shoe fits," Dorian replied under his breath, where only Zade could hear him. Then, a little louder, he added, "Since we don't have a camera anymore, I packed my drone in my backpack. Cassandra, your new job is to be a lookout and help watch for the thieves. I sure hope they've taken the bait. Okay?"

"Whatever!" she grunted.

The group continued walking in silence, only stopping whenever Dorian needed to consult the GPS unit. On the third such occasion, Dorian announced, "This is where Zade and I will need to start heading toward the road." He then handed the GPS unit to Sylvia saying, "It will take you right to the fake dig site. I've already programmed it to the correct waypoints. There should be plenty of good hiding places, too." And then, looking directly at the twins, warned, "Stealth is key! Please! Try to be as quiet as you can."

"I'll be fine as long as my stupid brother doesn't keep stepping on the back of my heels every other minute."

"Hey," Alexander began. "You're the one who—"

"ENOUGH!" Sylvia yelled. "Let's get one thing straight. I've been all over the world and met all kinds of people, but you two take the cake. I don't want to hear another word from either of you. Do you understand? I've got skills and you know I'm not afraid to use them!"

Confident that Sylvia had everything under control, Dorian grinned at her, mouthed the words 'Good luck', and headed toward the road with Zade.

The two boys said very little as they walked, both in deep thought about what was to come. The plan sounded good on paper, but they were fully aware that anything could go wrong tonight. The thieves might not show up. Someone could get hurt. The twins could get in a fight and alert the thieves that someone was watching them. Dozens of possibilities swirled through their minds.

Five-hundred feet from the edge of the road, a large gully forced them to turn right. This gully ran parallel to the road for miles, leveling out in only two places: (a) the entrance to the ranch, and (b) a quarter-mile stretch not far from where they stood. Knowing the thieves were unlikely

Dinosaurs, Diggers, and Thieves

to use the front entrance, he and Zade would stake out this location until they arrived.

Reaching their destination at last, Dorian whispered to Zade, "Okay. Hide somewhere over there until you hear the police sirens. Do you have the coordinates written down?"

"Check," Zade replied. "Be careful out there, man. Oh, by the way, what are you going to do? We've never really talked about that yet."

With a sly grin on his face, Dorian said, "Let's just say, I plan to burst their bubble and let the air out of their getaway plan." A knowing smile lit up Zade's face. "After I've done that, I'm going to use my drone to get that footage we need." Waving goodbye, Dorian turned around and walked back onto the ranch in the direction of where he anticipated the thieves would park their vehicle. Finding a small hill nearby, he climbed it and lay flat on his stomach.

Doubt once again started to creep into his mind. Perhaps they should have thought this through a little more. In an attempt to stop thinking this way, he decided to calm himself by looking at the stars he was supposed to be showing the others. Turning onto his back, he gazed up into the night sky. One thing was for sure: he knew he would never grow tired of this view. Nothing in New York City could compare to this.

The sound of tires on gravel jolted him out of his revelry. Rolling back onto his belly, he looked down to see a black shape slowly inching along the dirt road. From what he could tell, it appeared to be an SUV of some sort. Its headlights were off and the driver was driving painfully slow in an attempt to be quiet. When it finally stopped 100 yards from where he lay, two people exited the vehicle. Evidently the interior lights had been disabled, so he couldn't make out whether they were men or women, short or tall, fat or skinny. Stealthily, the two individuals moved in the direction of the pond.

Dorian made himself wait a full five minutes before creeping toward the getaway car. His senses were on alert and his heart was pounding. Quietly, he unzipped his backpack and pulled out the screwdriver he had brought with him. His plan was to depress the tire valve of each tire so that the air would seep out. If that didn't work, he would use the sharp knife he had borrowed from Jose.

Before getting started, Dorian took a moment to peer inside the vehicle. In the middle row he could see buckets, shovels, boxes of what appeared to be plaster, gloves, and several unrecognizable tools. Walking around to the cargo area in the back, the tinted windows partially blocked his view. He could make out a large, oddly shaped object, but wasn't sure what he was looking at. Suspecting it might be a part of Victoria, he attempted to open the tailgate. Unfortunately, it was locked tight.

Walking back around to the middle of the vehicle, he carefully lifted the handle of the door and crawled inside. Kneeling on the middle seat, he peered into the back. There, as plain as day, were two oblong objects crudely wrapped in plaster. One was half the size of the other, stretching about two feet long by one foot wide. This, Dorian knew, must contain Victoria's skull. He had no idea how heavy it would be, but he was determined to find out. Maneuvering himself into a good position, he bent over the second row of seats and tried to lift it. It was much heavier than he had feared. Straining to get a better grip, he tried again. Unsuccessful once more, he knew there was no way he was going to be able to lift it over the seat by himself.

Three loud explosions in the distance jolted Dorian from his thoughts. Looking out the front windshield, he saw a massive spider web of red, green, and blue sparks spreading across the sky. The fireworks were so unexpected that Dorian momentarily forgot where he was and what he was doing. It was the sound of heavy footsteps rapidly coming toward him that brought him back to the present. Fear gripped him like a vice and he did the only thing he could think to do. He climbed over the back seat and lay down next to the skeleton in an attempt to hide.

Chapter Eighteen

Back at the ranch house, Eric was enjoying a nice plate of freshly baked cookies while sitting on the couch with his ankle propped up on a pillow. Susan had been a surprisingly good card player and his ego was grateful for a break from his string of defeats. The extra attention he was getting from Susan this evening left him feeling mixed emotions. He appreciated being taken care of this way, but it also made him miss his own mother. In many ways, he was coming to realize that he would never be the same. Life would go on and the pain would weaken, but there would always be a hole in his heart that could only be filled by his mom.

As soon as Eric finished his cookies, Susan collected the empty plate and headed into the kitchen to do the dishes. This gave Eric the perfect opportunity to reach between the cushions of the couch, pull out the radio he had hidden there, and check to see if it was still working. So much time had passed since the others had left that he was beginning to worry. Seeing the little red light on the top glowing brightly calmed his fears and he returned it to its hiding place.

Walking back into the front room, Susan asked if he was up for another game of cards. Eric politely declined and so she grabbed the remote control for the television and handed it to him. "No problem! How about some TV?" she asked. "We only get three channels, but you might find something interesting. I'm going to read for a while in the other room, if you don't mind. Just holler if you need anything. Okay?"

"Yes ma'am," said Eric, taking the remote from her hand. Just as he was about to turn it on, something bright and colorful outside the front window caught his attention. Three large fireworks, a few seconds apart, exploded into view and slowly faded away.

Susan had seen them as well and ran over to the window to get a closer look. "How beautiful!" she exclaimed. "What a treat!"

Eric wasn't so sure about that. Alarm bells were going off in his head due to the fact that fireworks were not a part of the master plan. Weighing his options, he decided to take the risk and reached down to retrieve the radio once more.

Witnessing this, Susan asked, "Where did that come from?"

Choosing to ignore her question for the moment, Eric examined it more carefully and realized why he had not heard from the group. Somehow, he had accidentally changed the channel while stuffing it between the cushions. Quickly flipping it back to the correct channel, he heard Alexander's panicked voice shouting, "Eric! Where are you? Eric! Are you there? Is this thing working?"

His heart pounding, he pressed the talk button and responded. "This is Eric! What's going on?" He could not believe he had made such a stupid mistake!

Alexander only had to say three words before Eric dropped the radio and ran to the house phone. "Call the sheriff!"

Not surprisingly, Tom, Bill, and Jose had also seen the fireworks. "Did they say anything about setting off firecrackers tonight?" Tom asked Bill. "Those look pretty close."

"No. Not that I remember," Bill replied. Glancing down at his watch he added, "Hey, it's after eleven o'clock, too! Shouldn't they be headed back to town by now? And, by the way, where are the night watchmen? They should already be here."

"You're right," Tom replied. "Why don't you contact Susan on the radio and see if they've called to say they are running late or something?"

In an effort to keep the plan on track, Jose interjected, "Oh, you don't need to do that. I was thinking about leaving anyway. I'm really tired. I'll just go and talk to her myself."

"Don't be silly!" said Tom. "No one should walk out here alone in the dark."

"Ummm," Bill interrupted. "Has anyone seen the radio lately?"

Tom found it a few minutes later under one of the folding chairs they had brought with them. "I hope no one has been trying to contact us," he exclaimed. "Whoever had it last must have turned the volume down on accident."

"It wasn't me," Bill replied. "I picked it up from the front seat of the truck when we had to squeeze Jose in and I handed it to him to hold. Anyway, it doesn't matter now. I better call Susan right away."

Tom handed the radio to Bill who then walked several yards away to radio his wife. Susan replied almost immediately, her voice dripping with concern. "This is Susan and you better tell me the truth, Bill. Did you two know about this?"

Dinosaurs, Diggers, and Thieves

Not quite comprehending what she was referring to, Bill asked, "Did we know about what?"

"I'm not sure yet," she huffed. "All I know is Eric just called the sheriff. I have a feeling there hasn't been any stargazing going on after all!"

Bill swiveled on the spot, charged toward Jose, and demanded, "Start talking, amigo!"

Chapter Nineteen

As instructed, Zade remained hidden near the road in order to listen for the sound of police sirens. He occupied himself by imagining what it would be like to go to college in a couple years. He would miss his family, but couldn't wait for the intellectual challenge of the whole experience.

The sound of the fireworks took him off guard. Peeking over the edge of the gully he was hiding in, he saw movement near the SUV. He was unable to tell what was happening, but the engine roaring to life signaled something was wrong. Soon, the vehicle began to move over the bumpy terrain in the direction of the road. For a few seconds, it almost looked as if it was headed straight toward him. No, he suddenly realized, it *was* heading straight for him. Zade dove to his right and then scrambled back up just in time to see the driver course-correct, hit a small boulder, engage four-wheel drive, and then lurch back onto the road. Once on the flat surface, the SUV sped at top speed away in the opposite direction of Saddle Creek.

After the shock of the moment wore off, Zade began to wonder why Dorian hadn't let the air out of the tires as planned. Then it hit him. Maybe Dorian was in trouble. Climbing out of the ditch, he ran in the direction Dorian had walked several minutes earlier.

"Dorian?" he yelled.

No answer.

"Dorian?" he screamed a little louder. "Where are you?"

Once again, no answer came in response. A quick scan of the area revealed only tire tracks and a small black object lying about 20 feet away. Picking it up, a sick feeling came over him. It was Dorian's backpack; he would have never left it behind willingly.

Unsure of what to do, Zade began to brainstorm his next move. Option one was to stay put and wait for the police. Not even knowing if the police had been contacted yet, he moved on to option two. He could run to the road and attempt to flag down a passing car. Realizing a car on this road at this time of night was highly unlikely, he moved on to option three.

Dinosaurs, Diggers, and Thieves

He could try to locate Cassandra, Alexander, and Sylvia; make sure they were okay; and hope one of them had a brilliant idea that would get them out of this mess. Not able to think of an option four, he began to race toward the pond.

Roughly a third of the way there, he stopped to catch his breath. Seeing this as a good opportunity to look inside the backpack for something useful, he spotted Dorian's drone right on top. He wasn't that familiar with how to operate a drone, but he was willing to give it a go. For a moment, he felt a sense of optimism. This was quickly squelched, however, by the realization that a truck going over 60 miles an hour could never be overtaken by a drone like this. At best, it could go about half that speed.

Without realizing it, he had begun walking back toward the street. Something kept pushing him forward until he was just a few feet from the roadside. Looking around – for what, he didn't know – he saw a small puddle of liquid. For one awful second he thought it might be blood. The darkness of the night kept him from telling what color it was, so he knelt down, put his finger in the liquid, and sniffed. Thankfully, it was only gasoline. The SUV's chaotic off-road journey back to the road had evidently caused a small leak in its gas tank. That optimistic feeling once again crept into Zade's chest. Thinking back to what he had learned the last few days about following the bone trail, he wondered if he could apply the same technique to follow a sporadic trail of dripping gasoline.

Just then, the sound of another vehicle rapidly approaching caught his attention. Zade's first thought was that the thieves were coming back. When it came into view, however, he was thrilled to see it was Tom's old Ford truck. It screeched to a halt less than a yard from where he stood.

Tom jumped out of the driver's side, yelling, "Zade! Are you okay? Where's Dorian?"

"I don't know," he replied. "Sylvia and the twins are back that way, but I don't know if anyone is hurt."

"They're safe," Tom confirmed. "We've talked to them on the radio and I told them to make their way back to the ranch house."

Bill and Jose joined the pair on the road after exiting the passenger side of the truck. "Where's Dorian?" Bill demanded, not hearing Zade's answer the first time.

Stammering, Zade struggled to get out the words. "They, uh, well, they must have taken him." He felt responsible in some way as the three men stared at him in shock. Getting up the courage to speak again, he added, "But, I think I know how to find them!"

Dorian lay perfectly still in the rear of the SUV. They had been traveling now for 10 or 15 minutes and he was grateful for every second he hadn't been spotted. He hoped the men would get to wherever they were going and he could secretly crawl out the back unnoticed. Holding his breath, he listened to their conversation.

"The whole thing was a setup," said the man in the driver's seat. "I wouldn't have thought they were smart enough to pull something like this off!"

"Well they did!" the second man responded angrily. "Now, we are in big trouble. The boss is going to ring your neck, Frank."

"*My* neck?" the driver said incredulously. "Why my neck, Sal? You're the one who got us into this mess!"

"Me?" the second man laughed. "I told you we should have checked out the rumors first. You're the one who insisted we go ahead anyway!"

"Well, you weren't on the phone either," Frank said defensively. "Those bratty twins told the boss all about it last night. That confirmed what I overheard Roxy, or whatever her name is, saying at the restaurant."

"I say we keep driving, take what we've got, and call it quits. Boss doesn't know our real names and..."

Dorian stopped paying attention after the "bratty twins" comment. His mind was racing. Had Cassandra and Alexander been in on the plot to steal the skeleton from the start? He knew they were spoiled rotten, but he didn't think they were criminals. Had they really been feeding information to these thugs? How could they?

Without warning, the SUV went off road again until finally slowing to a stop. Every muscle in Dorian's body tensed in anticipation of what might be coming. Both men then exited the vehicle, slamming the doors closed tightly. Carefully peaking over the back seat, he watched as they lumbered toward a little shack a few yards away. Intuitively, he knew this was probably his one and only chance to escape.

Just as Dorian began to make his move, the bigger of the two men stopped in his tracks and said, "Wait! We should probably move the skeleton in case someone goes snooping around tonight."

Dorian's heart stopped as he heard the sound of shoes on dirt and gravel heading back toward the vehicle. Taking a deep breath to steady himself, he decided to take advantage of the one card he still had left to play – the element of surprise. Slowly and quietly, he reached over and picked up one of the rock hammers lying next to Victoria's skull. Every second now felt like an eternity. He could hear the heavy breathing of the men right outside the back gate now. Next came the click of the handle being depressed and the first sight of space appearing between the bottom of the door and the bumper of the vehicle. Fresh cool air began to spill into the rear of the SUV and two big arms began reaching inside.

Chapter Twenty

Sylvia and the twins joined Eric and Susan at the ranch house, as Tom requested. The group had so many questions for each other that everyone seemed to be talking at once.

"Okay, okay. One at a time!" Eric insisted. "Sylvia, you first."

"Thanks," she said appreciatively. "First of all, I need to know. Is Dorian okay, and where are Tom and Bill?"

"We don't really know," Eric explained.

"That poor boy!" Sylvia replied, practically in tears. "He's going to be all right, though. He's smart and he'll know what to do. This is just like the time I was in Egypt on an archeological dig. I was taken hostage by three tomb raiders. I knew it wasn't me they were after. They wanted treasure. Once they got it, they dropped me off in town and sent me on my way. I went straight to the authorities, of course. You know? I never heard if they were ever apprehended."

Eric hoped Sylvia was right. He had not known Dorian for very long, but it seemed like they had been friends forever. The last thing he wanted was to lose someone else close to him. "What I really want to know," Eric said, "is what in the world were those fireworks about?"

"Well," Alexander began. "When you didn't answer our radio call, I did the only thing I could think of. I got them from the clearance section at the general store when I bought the radios. I guess they were left over from the Fourth of July. I hated to waste them this way, but it sure was fun seeing those men scramble for cover. It's a shame we didn't have Cassandra's camera. I think the one guy almost wet himself."

Grudgingly, Eric admitted, "That was actually great thinking, Alexander!"

"Don't act so surprised," he snorted in return.

Sylvia, noticing Cassandra was unusually quiet, asked, "Are you okay, honey?"

"No, I'm actually not," she whimpered. "I'm worried about Dorian!"

Somewhere outside of town, a trapped teenage boy prepared to make his escape. He lifted the hammer high over his head as the tailgate opened wider. Counting down, he whispered, "Three, two, one!" and then slammed the hammer down with a resounding WHAMMMM!

"AHHHHH!" screamed the man, grasping his right forearm with his uninjured hand.

Without waiting to see what would happen next, Dorian jumped out of the SUV and began to run. Unfortunately, the chase was over in a matter of seconds. The much larger uninjured man had been just a few feet away and grabbed Dorian like he was a tiny mouse.

"Who do we have here?" he bellowed, holding Dorian roughly by his collar. "By the looks of you, I'd say you're Bill's son. Am I right?"

"Let me go!" Dorian yelled while trying unsuccessfully to kick the man in the shins.

His feeble attempts at pulling free were laughable to the two men. "He's a feisty one, ain't he?" said the man with the injured arm. "Hold him still, Frank. No one hits me and gets away with it!"

When Dorian woke up, he was lying on the ground inside what must be the old shed he had seen earlier from the truck window. His hands were tied behind his back and a foul-smelling rag covered his mouth. The two men were pacing back and forth not far from where he lay. Rather than struggle and alert them to the fact he was awake, he lay as still as possible in order to listen to them talk.

"Could this day get any worse, Frank?" complained Sal.

"Don't tempt fate!" Frank warned. "Stranger things have happened."

"What do we do now?" Sal asked, almost pitifully. "I'm not going back to prison. You know how I feel about confined places."

"I know, I know. Calm down," Frank responded. "I'll think of something. Just give me a second." After several minutes of quiet pacing, Frank spoke again. "Well, I guess we should find out what the kid knows first."

Taking his cue from Frank, Sal walked over to Dorian and forcibly yanked the gag off his mouth. Thinking quickly, Dorian pretended to wake up and said in a drowsy voice, "Where am I? What's going on?"

"Scream and I'll give you something to scream about!" Sal demanded. Dorian could tell he meant business and did as he was told.

Frank was the next to speak. "So, what do you know, boy?"

"Well," Dorian said, taking the time to think before responding. "I don't know much, but I do know two men who are in serious trouble. Can you say the word felony?"

Dinosaurs, Diggers, and Thieves

Instantly, Sal's eyes widened and he looked at Frank again. "What's he talking about?"

"He's just trying to scare us," Frank replied. "But, it's not going to work!"

"Okay," Dorian replied nonchalantly. "If you say so."

His calm demeanor under the circumstances only served to worry Sal all the more. "You better be sure, Frank! Do you hear me? I'm not going back, no matter what!"

"Shut up, you idiot!" Frank commanded and then turned his attention to Dorian once more. "All right, Mr Smarty Pants, how did we commit a felony?"

Dorian was more than happy to explain. "Well, stealing from government property is a federal offense."

"We didn't, Mr Know-It-All," Frank replied. "We stole from Tom and your father."

Dorian was curious to know how Frank knew who he was, but decided to ask about that later. "That's what we wanted you to think," Dorian explained. "I guess you could say we set up a kind of sting operation. The bones you attempted to steal were not on Cretaceous Ranch. They were found just over the boundaries of the ranch on federal property. We're talking a couple years, not counting the kidnapping charges."

"Kidnapping, Frank?" Sal pleaded, unable to keep the panic out of his voice. "I knew I shouldn't have listened to you and taken this stupid job!"

Frank was beginning to lose patience with his partner in crime, but was trying to stay calm. Dorian took note of not only the words Frank was using but his tone of voice as well. This time, he sounded a lot less sure of himself when speaking. "We're fine, okay! Trust me, man. I've got this."

Sal, less than convinced, said, "He sounds like he knows what he's talking about to me. You told me stealing fossils would be easier than robbing banks and scamming old ladies. There were supposed to be no witnesses, remember? And, Mr C said that posing as night watchmen would take the suspicion off us! A lot of good that did, right Frank?"

"Say one more word, Sal!" Frank growled with his fist in his face. "Or, do you want to just go ahead and give the kid our social security numbers and fingerprints, too? You're saying too much, idiot!"

"What? What did I say?" Sal questioned.

Dorian was beginning to put two and two together. The boss's name was Mr C. This new tidbit in combination with the conversation he had overhead the men having back in the vehicle confirmed his suspicions. He would find a way to stop the thieves and their boss, but first he needed to convince Frank and Sal to let him go. Racking his brain for a plan, Dorian remembered an old 1940s movie his mother had made him watch. In it, the hero had to arrange for his own release from captivity by promising the thieves a lighter sentence. The case was about a stolen diamond and not a dinosaur, but it was close enough.

Sal remained inconsolable no matter what Frank said. "We're going down aren't we, Frank? There is no way out! It's over. Let's just get in the truck and drive to the border."

Frank had evidently reached his limit. In a flash, he slammed Sal against the wall and shouted, "Shut up! Shut up! Shut up!"

This did the trick. Sal looked stunned and did as he was told.

Dorian decided to take advantage of the silence and continued to sow dissension among the pair. "You're wrong, you know? There is a way out of this!"

"You shut up, too!" Frank barked. "I've heard enough out of you!"

Sal, regaining his powers of speech, sheepishly said, "Maybe we should hear him out. If he has a plan to help us, we should listen. Don't you think?"

Frank sighed dramatically and let his shoulders droop in defeat. "All right, Sal. You win." Then, he looked at Dorian and in a syrupy sweet voice said, "Go ahead, kid. Evidently my partner here thinks we should let the inmates run the asylum." Then he bowed low and said, "What is it you wish us to do, my liege?"

Dorian wasn't quite sure what liege meant, but he decided to go ahead anyway. "Well, I was just trying to say that right now, you two have the advantage."

"How's that, Mr Sherlock?" Frank asked skeptically.

Taking a second to craft his words carefully, Dorian said, "Well, first of all, Mr Connor doesn't know what's happened here yet." Their lack of reaction to his substitution of *Mr Connor* for *Mr C* filled in a lot of blanks for him. Unfortunately, it also created several new ones. Realizing this wasn't the time to ponder this, he went on. "Rest assured, though, he will soon. You have a short window in which to act. If I were you, I would turn myself in and—"

"No way!" Sal interrupted. "I'm not ever going back to jail. And, when I say never, I mean never! Don't you get it?"

"Let me finish," Dorian said in a reassuring tone. "If, and I do mean if, you turn yourselves in, you might have the opportunity to work out a deal in exchange for testifying against Mr Connor."

"You must be insane!" Sal ventured on. "You obviously don't know who we're dealing with here. He'd hunt us down like dogs!"

"Yep," Frank said, nodding in agreement. "You know it!"

"I just think—" Dorian began, but was silenced by a noise coming from outside the shed, a noise sounding like a giant mosquito, which he recognized instantly.

Chapter Twenty-One

"Do you really think you know how to find Dorian?" Bill replied eagerly to Zade. "How?"

"Well, look on the ground," Zade explained while pointing down at the slowly evaporating trail of gasoline on the pavement. "Somehow, probably when they ran over that boulder over there, the SUV's gas tank was punctured."

"So, what are you saying?" Tom asked. "Will we find them stuck on the side of the road somewhere with an empty fuel tank? You know those SUVs carry a lot of fuel, right? They could be anywhere by the time they run out."

"No, I have an even better idea," said Zade. Then he grabbed Dorian's drone and thrust it at the two men. "Here!"

Bill took the drone, but the confused expression on his face conveyed the message that he needed more details.

"Couldn't you use the camera on Dorian's drone to trace the gasoline trail right to the SUV's location?" Zade asked.

Comprehension dawning on him, Bill looked at Zade, shook him lightly by the shoulders, and said, "You're brilliant! Just brilliant!"

It was Tom this time who had the confused look on his face. "Ummm, but why do we need the drone?"

"It's going to be hard to spot a thin line of gasoline while looking through a windshield five feet from the ground. There are two of you, so one can drive the truck and the other can navigate the drone from the passenger seat. The video feed will show up right on your phone and you'll be able to get as close as you want to the ground."

Once again, Bill looked at Zade and said, "He's brilliant, I tell you!" Then, he launched the drone and the two men headed back to the truck.

Hollering after them, Jose said, "I'll walk back to the house with Zade. Ten cuidado!"

The drone hovered in front of the truck like a hummingbird near a flower while the men strategized.

"Okay, Tom," Bill said. "Whatever you do, please don't drive faster than the drone. And, if I say stop, please stop immediately. We don't want to run it over. That would be a disaster."

"Got it," Tom agreed. "I'll make sure to stay a good six to ten feet back."

"Perfect! Are you ready?" asked Bill.

"Ready or not," Tom said and then started the engine.

Both the drone and the truck began to move forward. It took a while for the two men to coordinate their movements and Bill kept muttering impatiently, "Come on! Come on!" every time the truck had to slow down or the drone lost its way.

Tom couldn't imagine how he would be feeling if it were Eric instead of Dorian. He had already lost his wife and he would never be able to handle losing his son. Not knowing what to say to Bill, he encouraged him as much as possible by saying things like, "It's going to be okay," and, "Hang in there, buddy!" He also reminded Bill that the closer they got to the SUV, the fresher the gasoline trail would become. That would make their task easier as time went on.

They passed only two other vehicles the whole time and might have driven right by the SUV parked some distance from the side of the road if it hadn't been for Tom having to sneeze. Thankfully, luck was on their side. He had just turned his head away from Bill in order to cover his mouth and nose when he noticed a small structure not much larger than a tool shed about 50 yards from the road. It was too small to be someone's home, yet there was a vehicle parked nearby in the middle of the night.

"Look!" Tom said excitedly, slowing the truck to a stop.

"What? What do you see?" Bill asked.

"Look over there," Tom pointed. "Do you think that could be the SUV we're looking for?"

"I don't know, but we should definitely check it out, though," Bill said. "I'm a firm believer in serendipity."

"I agree," replied Tom. "But, let's use the drone just in case. We don't know if they are armed. Sound okay to you?"

"Absolutely," Bill said, already maneuvering the drone directly toward the building on the hill.

Chapter Twenty-Two

Hearing that sound caused hope to swell in Dorian's chest. Acting quickly, he started talking a bit louder than necessary in hopes that the men wouldn't hear the noise too. It did not work.

"Hush!" Frank barked. "What is that?"

Sal ran to the door and peeked outside. "There's something out there, but I can't see what it is."

"Get out of the way," Frank yelled, pulling Sal back so he could have a look himself. Opening the door quite a bit wider, he caught a glimpse of a truck he recognized parked on the side of the road. "You've got to be kidding me! It's Tom," he said in disbelief.

"How'd he find us?" Sal gasped. "Maybe we should do as the kid said. The police probably would go easier on us. We're small fry compared to Mr C."

"No, you idiot!" Frank yelled. "I thought you said you didn't want to go back to prison? Plus, the police aren't even here. It's just Tom and probably Bill. We can take them with our hands tied behind our backs."

"Maybe," Dorian said, "but I bet you anything the police are on their way. I promise to tell them you didn't kidnap me and it was all a mistake if you let me go. Plus, you'll have a lot of bargaining power if you snitch on Mr Connor."

"The kid's right," Sal agreed. "I think it might work."

"I'm in charge and I say no!" Frank yelled. "No, sir. I've got a better idea."

"What, Frank? Please don't do anything stupid," Sal pleaded. "What are you going to do, Frank, huh?"

"Make a run for it," he replied and then commanded Sal to untie Dorian.

He did what he was told and asked, "Now what?"

"Get to the SUV and bring him with us!"

DINOSAURS TO DRONES

Dorian found himself being half dragged, half carried back to the SUV. Upon arrival, he was thrown onto the floor of the middle row of seats and held down by Sal's big feet. For one brief moment he had dared to believe his nightmare was over. How foolish he had been.

"Hurry!" Sal screamed. "They're coming!"

Frank was too busy jamming the key into the ignition and backing up the vehicle to answer. If he didn't reach the fork in the dirt path before Tom's truck arrived, they would be trapped between the shed and the hills on either side.

Tom and Bill sped toward the trail that led uphill to the shed as soon as they realized they had been spotted. Tom wrenched the steering wheel to the right as hard as he could, launching the truck onto the trail with a screeching of tires.

"We got them now!" Tom proclaimed.

"Hurry!" Bill pleaded. "It looks like the path forks up ahead. If we get there before they do, we can block their escape route!"

"Here goes nothing!" Tom said and then pushed the gas pedal to the floor.

An onlooker would have seen nothing but two long plumes of dust racing toward each other from opposite directions. The two vehicles were on a collision course and it was anyone's guess as to who would reach the fork first. Once the dust cleared, it was all too obvious who had been faster.

"YES!!!" screamed Frank at the top of his lungs. "See, Sal? Didn't I say you should listen to me?"

Sal waited to respond until the SUV stopped bouncing and was back on smooth pavement. "You were right, Frank. I'm sorry. Really sorry for doubting you."

Dorian couldn't see what had just occurred, but he sure could feel it. He had always been prone to car sickness, but this took the cake.

Frank started whistling and humming and seemed energized by their close call. "Where to now, old pal? Where to now?" he asked.

"All I know is as far away as you can get from here."

"Truer words have never been said!" Frank laughed.

Just then, a high-pitched beep came from the SUV's dashboard. "What was that?" Sal asked.

"Ahhh, it's nothing," Frank said, not wanting anything to dampen his mood. "We need gas, but we still have at least another gallon until it reaches E. I think there's a gas station about five miles from here. We've got plenty, my friend. Plenty!"

From Dorian's position on the floor, he couldn't tell exactly how fast they were going, but the wind noise indicated pretty fast. About three minutes later, the SUV's engine began to sputter and slow down. This created quite a rocking motion, which served to upset Dorian's stomach even more.

"Stop playing around," Sal laughed. "That's not funny."

"I'm not trying to trick you," Frank said convincingly. "Somethings wrong with the engine."

Finally, the SUV's engine stopped completely and it rolled to a stop on the side of the road. "Plenty, huh?" Sal said. "Plenty of gas until it gets to zero, huh? NOW WHAT, FRANK?"

"I don't understand it," Frank replied. "There's no way we are out of gas. We've driven this route many times and should have another 20 or 25 miles."

"Evidently, not this time," Sal replied sarcastically. The two men started hitting and shoving each other between the seats and would have continued until someone got hurt, but they were interrupted by flashing red and blue lights.

"Nooooooo!" whaled Sal. "This can't be happening to me!"

"To you?" Frank asked sarcastically. "I see how you are. Only worry about the big numero uno."

"Come out with your hands up," came a voice over a loudspeaker mounted on the police car.

Sal began pleading for Frank to do what Dorian had suggested. He seemed so pitiful that even Dorian began to feel sorry for him.

"You let me do the talking for both of us," Frank ordered. "Okay?"

"Okay," Sal blubbered, with tears in his eyes.

"And, Dorian," Frank continued. "You promise you'll tell them we didn't intentionally kidnap you?"

Getting up from the floor, Dorian answered, "Cross my heart, hope to die!"

"I said, come out with your hands up!" the police officer demanded once more.

Before Dorian knew what was happening, Frank and Sal were on the ground and surrounded by three officers with their guns drawn. Bill came running toward Dorian and gave him a huge hug. "Are you all right, son?" he said with panic in his voice.

"I'm fine, Dad," Dorian replied. "And, I'm so sorry. I'll never disobey you again."

"We'll see how long that lasts," Bill joked while choking back tears. "Don't worry. We'll talk about your punishment later."

Tom was standing behind the father and son, letting them have their moment. When the hug was over, he walked up to Dorian, mussed his hair,

and said, "Glad to see you're okay, buddy! I don't know what we are going to do with you two boys!"

"Oh, I almost forgot," Dorian said excitedly. "Follow me!" Then he led the men to the rear of the SUV. "There's something in here that belongs to you!"

Chapter Twenty-Three

Tom was overjoyed when he saw the hadrosaur's missing pieces laying in the back of the SUV. You would have thought it was Christmas, his birthday, and Independence Day all rolled into one. "I know we should be furious. You put yourself in a lot of danger, but…thank you. The whole town thanks you!"

"It wasn't just me," Dorian replied. "It was everyone. Eric, Sylvia, Zade, Jose, and…"

Dorian stopped himself before adding "the twins." Although it was too awful to consider, the evidence said otherwise. *Exhibit A*: The twins talked to their father every night on the phone. *Exhibit B*: Mr Connor was the one who hired the security guards. *Exhibit C*: There were two people willing and able to testify against Mr Connor who were currently being arrested in front of them. *Exhibit D*: Well, a good lawyer wouldn't need an exhibit D.

Just then, something his mother often said came to mind. "Give others the benefit of the doubt. Seeing the good in others always brings out the good in you." Pondering this a moment, Dorian realized it was very possible that Cassandra and Alexander hadn't known they were helping their father. Someone like Mr Connor could have easily used his own children to gather inside information. The more he thought about it, the more he realized how smart that would be. The twins would have plausible deniability and he would come out smelling like a rose. Dorian made up his mind right then to refrain from drawing conclusions until he had a chance to talk to them himself.

After giving his statement to the police, Bill and Tom took Dorian back to the ranch. Eric and the others were overjoyed when Dorian walked in the door. There was a tremendous amount of cheering, high-fiving, and hugs all around. Even Cassandra and Alexander showed a little emotion.

Susan pushed her way to the front of the crowd, grabbed her son, and said, "I don't know what I'm going to do with you, young man!" Tears were streaming down her face as she held him tight. "Don't you ever do this to me again! Do you hear me?"

Dorian smiled at her, kissed her on the cheek, and said, "I promise!"

Next, each person took turns telling the events of the night from their point of view. Dorian waited to go last in order to watch the twins' reactions to the news that their father had been the mastermind. Cassandra's tears and Alexander's adamant denials told him all he needed to know. The twins were completely innocent.

Shortly after 2:00 a.m., Susan announced it was time for bed. It was decided that everyone would sleep at the ranch house for the night and go home in the morning. The stress of the day had worn Dorian out and he was asleep before his head hit the pillow.

The sound of hushed whispers and a gurgling coffee pot woke Dorian up the next day. It was almost noon and everyone had left except for Tom and Eric. The group was huddled together around the kitchen table in deep conversation.

"Well, welcome to the land of the living, son!" Bill teased, spotting Dorian peeking around the corner.

"Morning," Dorian said, yawning loudly. "What's going on? Any news?"

"Well, there is actually," Bill began. "Frank and Sal, AKA our former night watchmen, took a deal to do six months in exchange for testifying against Mr Connor. A police officer is due to arrive at his primary residence in California sometime this afternoon to arrest him on charges of stealing from government property, racketeering, trespassing, and a dozen other crimes."

"Wow!" Dorian replied. "I never thought I'd be saying this, but I feel badly for the twins. It's one thing to have an absent father who's on business trips all the time. It's quite another to know your father is a criminal and a felon. What will happen to them?"

"I'm not sure, honey," answered Susan. "I imagine they have other relatives they can stay with and—"

Her comment was interrupted by the telephone ringing. Bill, who had been closest to the phone, answered it. "Hello?...Yes, he's here. Who should I say is calling?" Then he pointed the phone at Dorian and said, "It's for you."

Not knowing who could possibly be calling him, Dorian took the phone and said, "This is Dorian."

A woman with a pleasant but official-sounding voice said, "My name is Brooke Davidson and I work with the Bureau of Land Management. We need to talk to you about the fossil you helped recover last evening."

"Sure," Dorian replied. "But, I think you should speak to Tom. He's the paleontologist who actually discovered the fossil on my great-uncle's property a while ago."

Handing the phone to Tom, the others listened to his side of the conversation. "Hello, this is Tom…Ahuh…Yes…well, I can send you the GPS coordinates…How do you already have them?…Oh really!…Yes, I am sure it is on private land…Because Philip lived on the land for decades and…No, but…He showed me a map of his land…Are you sure?…There is no way you made a mistake?…Well, you don't understand what this means to our community…Tomorrow? I guess so. I'll meet you at the train station. What time?…9:00 a.m. Bye."

Tom hung up the phone and turned around with a devastated look on his face.

"What's wrong?" Eric asked.

"The Bureau of Land Management was notified about Victoria by the state police. They obtained the GPS coordinates from the thieves and, according to their preliminary research, have questions about whether or not the specimen is really on Philip's land. They are coming here tomorrow to investigate."

"*No* way!" Eric yelled. "They think we stole Victoria? We would never do something like that!"

"Calm down, son," Tom urged. "They don't think we stole it. They have reason to believe Philip's map was wrong."

Dorian and the rest of the group fell silent and stared at each other in dismay.

Chapter Twenty-Four

Time seemed to slow down as the group waited for their unwanted visitor from the Bureau of Land Management to arrive. In order to keep themselves from falling into despair, they decided to use every minute they had to collect evidence and build a case establishing Philip's ownership of Victoria. Dorian and Eric spent hours searching the files stacked in Philip's dining room, and Tom made phone calls to lawyers in Helena, seeking legal counsel. Bill and Susan decided to drive to the courthouse and request copies of any deeds or other historical documents that would help trace ownership back to the time of the Homestead Act of 1862. Unfortunately, most of their efforts proved fruitless.

At last, 9:00 a.m. the following day arrived. The train blared its horn just as it had the day Dorian and his parents arrived in Saddle Creek. Today the sound no longer startled them, but instead served as a harbinger of bad news. They were at the mercy of the federal government now. A tall woman in a blue pantsuit exited the train, accompanied by a white-haired man in his late fifties.

Tom was the first to greet them, saying politely, "Hello. I'm Tom, the man you spoke with on the phone yesterday."

"Ahhh," the older man said with a quirky smile on his face. "I imagine you are not too happy to see us today, are you?"

"Well, now that you mention it," Tom replied. "We are a little perplexed, Mr..."

"It's actually Doctor," the man corrected. "I'm Dr Wainwright. Pleased to make your acquaintance." The man took turns shaking each person's hand as introductions were made all around.

"Why don't we go over to Skinny's Pizza," suggested Tom. "We can order a cold drink and talk a little more privately."

"Lead the way," Dr Wainwright replied.

Dinosaurs, Diggers, and Thieves

The group walked in awkward silence until they reached the restaurant. Tom opened the door and escorted everyone to a couple tables in the corner. Unlike Tom, the two boys were having a hard time concealing their anger and suspicion. The man seemed completely unfazed, however, by the glares they were sending his way.

"You were right," Dr Wainwright said to Tom. "This is a much better place to talk. Thank you for suggesting it."

It was Bill who spoke next. "Please, Doctor. Spare us the pleasantries and tell us what brings you here today."

The man simply nodded and took his time saying, "I suppose that would be best. Brooke, would you care to elaborate?"

"Not at all," she offered. "I am a grad student currently conducting a research study for the Bureau of Land Management. My specialty is satellite imagery and telemetry. Dr Wainwright, a high-ranking geologist for the BLM, was notified about the stolen fossil yesterday and subsequently obtained the GPS location for the original dig site. I happened to be streaming data from a satellite I use to track the migratory path of antelope when he asked me to enter the coordinates into my database. He then superimposed a map displaying the boundaries of public lands in the area onto my screen and discovered something interesting. The line went right through the dig site."

"So, what does this mean?" Susan asked.

"What it means," Dr Wainwright replied, "put simply, is that Victoria may belong to the federal government."

"But, we have a map showing the boundaries of Philip's ranch right here," Dorian explained. "Eric marked the dig site with a green X. It is clearly inside the borders of the ranch."

"Well, that is why we are here," Dr Wainwright continued, "to get to the bottom of this once and for all. I assure you, I have no interest in taking something that rightfully belongs to you. On the other hand, it is my duty to protect the past and preserve for the future anything within my jurisdiction. The only way to verify if the dinosaur is on private or public land is for you to take us to the site."

"Well, there's no time like the present," Tom chirped. "I can't take the suspense any longer. Let's go."

One hour later all eight of them stood looking down at the back half of the headless dinosaur. Brooke got out her laptop and connected it to a satellite data receiver. She began to type and scroll through screen after screen as the others looked on.

DINOSAURS TO DRONES

"You see," Dr Wainwright explained. "Satellite GPS systems will soon be accurate within a few inches. They are pretty close to that now, but in a case like this, every inch counts."

"But, what about our map?" Dorian asked. "Doesn't it mean anything?"

"Hand-drawn maps and those created by land surveyors of the past are much less reliable. People were simply not capable of achieving the accuracy that we are today," he explained.

"We should have a verdict in just a minute," Brooke advised.

"Oh, I can't take the suspense!" Susan said anxiously.

"Me either," added Eric.

Brooke's computer beeped loudly three times in succession. "That tells me the program has finished running its analysis. Okay, it's rendering the image now."

Dorian's heart dropped when he saw what was on the screen.

Chapter Twenty-Five

Brooke's computer screen showed exactly what Dorian, Tom, and the others feared. The boundary line did indeed intersect with Victoria's skeleton. Two-thirds of the skeleton lay on Philip's land and one-third lay on public land.

"I'm just devastated," Tom confessed. "All the time and effort we spent on this specimen to now see it taken away? I can't comprehend this right now."

"Hold your horses, or should I say hadrosaurs," Dr Wainwright interjected. "Nothing has been decided as of yet. This situation is, well, unprecedented, so I will need to confer with my colleagues. One thing I can promise you, though, is that you will be compensated for your portion of the dinosaur, if it comes to that."

"I don't want your money!" Tom passionately explained. "We want Victoria! We want to see her displayed in our very own museum one day. We want to see tourists arriving by Amtrak. We want to see our downtown alive again. We want to see our kids proud to say they are from Saddle Creek. It's not about personal gain or fame or riches."

Dr Wainwright studied Tom closely, not saying a word. A full minute later he finally responded. "I'll take that under advisement. If you will excuse me, I have a phone call to make. This shouldn't take long."

Contrary to his promise, Dr Wainwright spent almost an hour talking, and at some points arguing, on the phone while the others looked on. Despite their best efforts, he was too far away for anyone to hear what was being said. Only a smattering of words and phrases could be heard, like *matter of principle*, *letter of the law*, and *eminent domain*. None of these words made sense to Dorian so he did not quite know what to think.

Finally, Dr Wainwright rejoined the group, looking somber. "Well," he began, "I have good news and bad news. The good news is, due to the fact that hadrosaurs are not that uncommon and a majority of the skeleton is on Philip's land, we are open to ceding our interest in the skeleton to you."

"That's awesome!" Eric cheered.

"Before you celebrate," Dr Wainwright interrupted. "I want to share with you the bad news. We will only relinquish control of the skeleton if a proper facility is constructed in the next 90 days. If not, we will promptly move the skeleton to the Museum of the Rockies for further study."

"But, that's simply not possible!" Tom explained. "We don't have that kind of money. And, what does an approved facility even mean?"

"The building will need to be climate controlled, provide adequate security to prevent any further fossil poaching, and include all the materials necessary for proper scientific study to occur," said Dr Wainwright.

"There's just no way we can come up with the money to build a whole new building in the next 90 days," Tom replied disappointedly. "You just don't know how big of an ask that really is!"

"What if we didn't build a *new* building?" Eric inquired. "What if we fix up a building already owned by the town?"

Tom gave his son a quizzical look and said, "I've told you before, Eric, that all of the empty shops downtown are privately owned and mortgaged to the hilt. The owners couldn't give them to us even if they wanted to."

"What if it's not a shop at all?" Eric said, grinning from ear to ear. "Why couldn't we use the train station?"

"That dump?" Dorian asked incredulously.

"Yes, that dump!" Eric countered. "It already has indoor plumbing, an air conditioner, and a waiting room big enough to hold a dinosaur skeleton."

"True," Tom agreed. "But, it would take upwards of $20,000 to repair the roof, replace the sagging floor, add security cameras, and fix anything else we might find. I don't have that kind of money and don't really know anyone who does. Do any of you?" Tom asked, looking from one person to the next around the circle.

When Tom's eyes landed on Dorian, he surprised everyone by saying, "Yes, Tom. I actually do!"

Chapter Twenty-Six

Today would be the last day the twins would be volunteering. Their grandmother from Florida had agreed to look after them during the trial that would no doubt go on for months. Given the new accelerated timetable, the other diggers had consented to stay on past their agreed-upon stays to help finish unearthing the rest of Victoria. This meant removing the remaining rock from the fossil, applying a plaster cast, carefully pedestaling it so it could be moved, and then transporting it to the soon-to-be revamped train station.

When the van pulled up to the dig site, Dorian noticed the twins lacked their usual vigor. They didn't push and shove or argue about who would be first. Instead, they calmly walked over to the circle and waited for instructions. There was something very odd about seeing them so quiet. It just wasn't normal.

Tom was the first to speak. "Thank you again, Cassandra and Alexander! None of this would be possible if it weren't for your gift."

"It was nothing," Alexander shrugged. "A couple years of allowance and interest from our savings accounts? That's just chump change."

"We hold no hard feelings against either of you," Tom assured them, and the others echoed in agreement. "You two are welcome to come back anytime."

This was the first time Dorian could remember ever seeing either of them genuinely smile. Deep inside, they weren't that bad after all. At the end of the eight-hour workday, everyone escorted the twins to the train platform. While waiting for the train, Dorian peered through the windows of the old station, imagining what it would look like in just a couple months as the "Philip McAllister and Family Paleontology Museum of Saddle Creek, Montana."

When the train finally arrived, the twins gathered their belongings and began to board. Just before disappearing through the door of their train car, Eric called out, "Hey, Cassandra! Watch out for those horned toads. You know they have them in Florida, too, right?"

She smiled brightly, waved goodbye, and disappeared inside. Over dinner that night at Skinny Joe's Pizza, Dorian took time to look around at the people sitting at his table. They were different from each other in so many ways: age, race, gender, even culture. But, they had one thing in common. They had been brought together on a search for excitement and discovery. They had found their excitement, oh yes, but more importantly, they had made discoveries. Discoveries about themselves and each other. Dorian hoped he would always have friends like this around him. He smiled to himself, realizing that you never know what you'll find when you give people, and sometimes places, a chance.

THE END

APPENDIX

This story was inspired by the author's participation in an actual dinosaur dig over a decade ago. A newspaper article written about this experience at the time has been included on the next page (Figure A.2). The author wishes to thank the Judith River Dinosaur Institute and the Dayton Daily News as well.

Figure A.2

Callahan, Beth (2002, October 31). Teacher realizes dinosaur dreams. *Dayton Daily News*, page 34.

References

Arnold, D. (2009). *Global warming and the dinosaurs*. Clarion Books.
Baby Professor. (2017). *How drones work*. Baby Professor.
Cash, R. (2016). *Self-regulation in the classroom*. Free Spirit Press.
Clinton, C. (2019). *She persisted*. Philomel Books.
CNN Money. (2017, March). U.S. drone registrations skyrocket to 770,000. Retrieved from (https://fox2now.com/news/u-s-drone-registrations-skyrocket-to-770000/)
Cox, A. (2007). *No mind left behind: Understanding and fostering executive control*. Perigee Trade.
DK. (2014). *Knowledge encyclopedia: Dinosaurs*. D.K. Children.
Huebner, D. (2005). *What to do when you worry too much*. Magination Press.
Jenkins, S. (2017). *Apex predators: The world's deadliest hunters, past and present*. HMH Books for Young Readers.
Nelson-Spickert, D. (2010). *Earthsteps: A rock's journey through time*. Fulcrum Publishing.
Oppel, K. (2016). *Every hidden thing*. Simon and Schuster.
Perkins, S. (2017, March). Dinosaur family tree poised for colossal shake-up. *Nature Magazine*.

Schilling, D. (2013, April). Knowledge doubling every 12 months, soon to be every 12 hours. Retrived from (https://www.industrytap.com/knowledge-doubling-every-12-months-soon-to-be-every-12-hours/3950)

Sousa, D. (2002). *How the gifted brain learns*. Corwin Press.

VanTassel-Baska, J., & Little, C. (2023). *Content based curriculum for advanced learners*. Routledge Press.

Wilder, L. I. (2008). *The long winter*. Harper Collins.

Witmer, L. M. (1995). The extant phylogenetic bracket and the importance of reconstructing soft tissues in fossils. In J. J. Thomason (Ed.), *Functional morphology in vertebrate paleontology* (pp. 19–33). Cambridge University Press.

Master Materials List

Note: This list does not include reproducibles indicated in each lesson plan.

Lesson 1

- One blank notebook for each student to use as a learning journal
- Markers
- Chart paper

Lesson 3

- Calculators
- Two or more yardsticks
- Four rulers

DINOSAURS TO DRONES

Lesson 4

- Sentence strips
- Tape

Lesson 5

- Small wooden dinosaur skeleton model with the pieces scrambled
- Highlighter

Lesson 8

- Two pieces of Elmer's foam board
- Scissors or knife
- Glue
- Toothpicks
- Bottle lid or poker chip

Lesson 9

- Dice

Lesson 11

- Small drone (if available)

Lesson 12

- Raw potato
- Sponge or okra
- Stamp pad
- Blank paper
- Cleaned chicken bone
- Real fossil (collected by students, purchased online, etc.)
- White, wheat, and rye bread
- Gummy worms or gummy bears
- Heavy books
- Paper towels
- Various books about paleontology

Master Materials List

Lesson 15

- Flashlight
- Ball
- *Earthsteps: A Rock's Journey through Time* by Diane Nelson Spickert

Lesson 18

- *Apex Predators: The World's Deadliest Hunters, Past and Present* by Steve Jenkins
- Dice

Lesson 20

- *How Drones Work* by Baby Professor

Lesson 21

- One 12-inch by 12-inch square of corrugated cardboard per person
- Scissors
- Glue
- Compass (the type used to draw circles)
- Ruler

Lesson 22

- Four straight pins per person

Lesson 23

- Gyroscope toy

Lesson 24

- Items to disassemble
- Screwdrivers of different sizes
- Goggles

Lesson 25

- Calculators

DINOSAURS TO DRONES

Lesson 27

▶ The book *She Persisted* by Chelsea Clinton

Lesson 29

▶ The book *Global Warming and the Dinosaurs* by Caroline Arnold

Lesson 30

▶ Materials needed to play the four chosen games
▶ A timer

About the Author

Jason S. McIntosh, Ph.D., is an experienced educator (27 years in the field) and a passionate advocate for gifted education. He earned his doctorate in Gifted, Creative, and Talented Studies at Purdue's Gifted Education Research Institute (GERI) in 2015 while working with Dr. Marcia Gentry to identify high-potential Dine, Lakota, and Ojibwa youth. Since his time at Purdue, Jason has served as a gifted coordinator and Director of Advanced Learning Experiences for several school districts in Arizona. He is now a Senior Instructional Designer for Goodwill of Central and Northern Arizona. In his free time, he enjoys traveling with his partner, reading YA literature, taking care of his 40-pound African spurred tortoise, and writing curriculum. In fact, Jason has authored eight NAGC Award-winning curriculum units (2016–2023) and hopes to write many more in the future. To find out more about his latest curriculum projects, please visit his website at www.notmoreofthesame.com.

For Product Safety Concerns and Information please contact our EU representative GPSR@taylorandfrancis.com
Taylor & Francis Verlag GmbH, Kaufingerstraße 24, 80331 München, Germany